THE LIBRARY OF
PHILOSOPHY AND THEOLOGY

Edited by

JOHN MCINTYRE AND IAN T. RAMSEY

THE STUDY OF RELIGIOUS LANGUAGE

Titles available

THE ABSOLUTENESS OF CHRISTIANITY, by Ernst Troeltsch

BASIC QUESTIONS IN THEOLOGY, Vols. I and II, by Wolfhart Pannenberg

CHRIST THE CRISIS, by Friedrich Gogarten

CHRISTIAN ETHICS AND CONTEMPORARY PHILOSOPHY, edited by Ian T. Ramsey

CREATIVE SYNTHESIS AND PHILOSOPHIC METHOD, by Charles Hartshorne

DO RELIGIOUS CLAIMS MAKE SENSE?, by Stuart C. Brown

FAITH AND UNDERSTANDING, by Rudolf Bultmann

KIERKEGAARD ON CHRIST AND CHRISTIAN COHERENCE, by Paul Sponheim

NORM AND CONTEXT IN CHRISTIAN ETHICS, edited by Paul Ramsey and Gene H. Outka

SCHLEIERMACHER ON CHRIST AND RELIGION, by Richard R. Niebuhr

THEISM AND EMPIRICISM, by A. Boyce Gibson

THEOLOGY AND METAPHYSICS, by James Richmond

TOWARDS A THEOLOGY OF INVOLVEMENT, A study of Ernst Troeltsch, by Benjamin A. Reist

THE STUDY OF
RELIGIOUS LANGUAGE

ANDERS JEFFNER

SCM PRESS LTD
BLOOMSBURY STREET LONDON

This book was printed with the help of a grant from the Swedish Humanistic Research Council.

A/200.1

334 01577 4
FIRST PUBLISHED 1972
© SCM PRESS LTD 1972
PRINTED IN GREAT BRITAIN BY
WESTERN PRINTING SERVICES LTD
BRISTOL

TO ANNA, KRISTINA AND ERIK

CONTENTS

Introduction   I

I   Terminological Remarks   3
    1 Definition of 'religious language' 33
    2 Analytical terminology 10

II   Religious Statements   20
    1 'The problematic set of religious sentences' 21
    2 Are any religious sentences members of the problematic set? 22
    3 Are any sentences belonging to the problematic set of religious sentences statements with their localization in the real world? 30
    4 Are some religious sentences in the problematic set direct statements with a localization other than the real world? 35
    5 Does the problematic set of religious sentences contain any indirect statements? 40
    6 Does any theory of metaphors or symbols or analogies or models solve the problem of religious statements? 52

III   Religious Expressions and Prescriptions   68
    1 Expressions of emotive and conative impulses in religious men 69
    2 Expressions ascribed to God or to supernatural beings 76
    3 Sentences expressing a 'perspective' 78
    4 Examples of problems raised by an emotive theory of value 80
    5 Additional questions concerning religious prescriptions 81

IV   Religious Performatives   88
    1 Conditions for the correct use of a performative 89
    2 The classification of religious performatives 90
    3 The analysis of religious performatives 92
    4 The gain in identifying and analysing performatives in religious language 98

V The Epistemological Basis   105

    1 Eschatological verification   107
    2 Religious experience   107
    3 Faith as interpretation   112
    4 A theory illustrating the ultimate choices in judging religious language   120

Index of Names   133

INTRODUCTION

SINCE THE middle of this century, a large number of books and articles have been written on the subject of what is termed 'religious language'. At present there is a bewildering array of disparate and contradictory theories in this field.[1] What is now needed, it seems, is an investigation of the criteria for a correct analysis of religious language. Questions of the following kind are too seldom raised in the discussion. What kind of analysis do philosophers provide? To what criteria are they appealing when they claim one analysis to be correct and another wrong? Are their criteria reasonable? The present book is designed to bring such questions into focus. We shall try to interpret existing theories of religious language in a way which makes clear how their validity or otherwise can be determined. We shall also try to establish what analytical methods are fruitful in different fields of the study of religious language. As a result, we hope to be able to indicate how far it is possible to acquire solid knowledge and reach probable hypotheses. In the course of our investigation, however, we will be bound to restrict our theme in a variety of respects.

When we study one of the existing theories of religious language, it is far from certain that we will understand immediately what the theory is about, what kind of theory it is, or how it is related to other, similar theories. The primary task, therefore, is to try to define the set of sentences about which the different theories of religious language may have something to

[1] There are many good collections of essays illustrating the different theories. The most recent one is Basil Mitchell (ed.), *The Philosophy of Religion*, Oxford University Press, Oxford 1971, which also contains a valuable bibliography.

say. Secondly, we need a terminology according to which these theories may be interpreted, making possible a comparison. In our first chapter we shall discuss the definition of a religious sentence, and introduce the necessary analytic terminology. Following the distinction made in Chapter I, we shall divide religious sentences into four main categories and investigate analyses of these categories of sentences in Chapters II, III and IV. In discussing the arguments for different analytical standpoints, we shall frequently find that certain specific philosophical theories concerning our knowledge of the world are of decisive importance for the outcome of the analysis. To complete our study, we must therefore discuss what kinds of statements can reasonably be made about the real world (Chapter V). We shall try to point out what decisions determine different epistemological standpoints. This will lead us to the fundamental questions relating to the truth of religion, and to the rationality of using a religious language.

I

TERMINOLOGICAL REMARKS

1. Definition of 'religious language'

Concentration on religious sentences A religious language can be seen as a number of interrelated written or spoken religious sentences, and this is the terminology we shall adopt. A sentence is a unit of words, arranged according to the grammatical rules of a given language, which is or could be terminated by a full stop, a question mark or an exclamation mark. This definition is not entirely satisfactory, but its imperfections will cause no difficulties in our particular context. If we could give an immediate definition of a religious language, then we could define a religious sentence as one of a number of sentences by which such a religious language is built up. This seems an extremely difficult task, so we shall begin at the other end and start by seeking a definition of religious sentences. After finding such a definition, we could go on to define a religious language as a language consisting of religious sentences co-ordinated according to certain rules. We shall concentrate on religious sentences, but we shall naturally not isolate the sentences from the system in which they are used.[1] Many existing theories of

[1] The reader must observe that it is an important limitation of our study not to discuss fully the rules through which the sentences in a certain religious language can be connected. It is also necessary to underline from the beginning the following quotation from Ninian Smart's book *Reasons and Faiths*, Routledge & Kegan Paul, London 1958, pp.165ff. 'The concepts alluded to in such propositions as "God exists" and "There is only one God and Mohammed is His Prophet", etc., are embedded in doctrinal schemes. They are not, in one sense of "simple", simple concepts since to understand them one has to pay attention to many, if not all, of the major assertions of the doctrinal scheme.' Cf. Antony Flew, *God and Philosophy*, Hutchinson, London 1966, pp.25ff.

religious language can be translated into theories concerning religious sentences.

Requirements of an appropriate definition   What kind of definition are we looking for? It cannot be a definition which simply states how the term 'religious sentence' is used in ordinary English. No such common use of the term exists which would enable us, by describing it, to establish a fairly stable border-line between religious and non-religious sentences. What we need is a stipulation which removes some of the vagueness of the term 'religious sentence', but which allows us to use it as far as possible in accordance with everyday language. Such a stipulative definition cannot be true or false, but it can be more or less convenient.

A definition is not, of course, convenient if it allows us to call a sentence religious which is obviously non-religious according to the ordinary use of the expression, or vice versa. We shall refer to this as 'the common-use requirement'.

It is more important to notice another requirement of the definition. Nothing must be introduced in the definiens which anticipates the analysis.[2] Suppose that I define a religious sentence as a sentence expressing an emotion of awe towards the world. It would not then be very illuminating if I should declare, as a result of an analysis, that religious sentences express emotions. We shall refer to the fault of the definition in this example as a 'lack of analytic neutrality'. The question of analytic neutrality deserves further comment.

Comments on analytic neutrality   Many essays on religious language seem to start from the assumption that we know intuitively what sentences are religious and what are not. The vagueness of the term sometimes does not matter. The analysis may concern sentences of such a nature that no one could doubt that they are religious. This is the case, for example, in the famous

[2] Cf. William T. Blackstone, *The Problem of Religious Knowledge*, Prentice-Hall, Inc., Englewood Cliffs, N. J. 1963, p.43. Blackstone's book is, according to my evaluation, one of the clearest commentaries on the debate about religious knowledge. On some fundamental points, however, my position is different from Blackstone's. This comes to light especially in Chapter V.

paper by R. B. Braithwaite in which he states that religious sentences when seen in their usual context are primarily used to express a commitment to a certain way of life.[3] Even in such cases, however, the study of an essay or article may leave the reader in doubt as to whether the underlying definition of a religious sentence was analytically neutral or not. Suppose that an opponent of Braithwaite were to give an example of a religious sentence – or assertion, as Braithwaite calls it – which for a specific person is totally unrelated to his way of life. This person would, for instance, be a man who had always tried to follow Christian ethics; one day he also comes to believe something of the Christian creed and says 'God created the world', without this affecting his life in any way. Such a situation cannot, without an empirical test, be said to be uncommon or atypical. Supposing it to be common, should it then count against Braithwaite's theory, or should we say that the sentence 'God created the world' is not a true religious sentence in this situation? We cannot obtain a definite answer from Braithwaite's short article, but if a defender of Braithwaite were to adopt the second alternative, then we could say that the theory, since it excludes such a sentence from religious language, is not based on an analytically neutral definition.

Some definitions suggested by different philosophers We will now proceed to discuss some possible types of definitions of a religious sentence in order to find one we can accept.[4]

An easy way out would be to define religious sentences with reference to certain documents in which they can be found – for instance the Bible. Such a definition, however, can never satisfy the common-use requirement. It would at the very least be too narrow. Many sentences that are obviously religious – for example those spoken by a man in a free prayer to God – will be excluded by this definition.

[3] R. B. Braithwaite, *An Empiricist's View of the Nature of Religious Belief*, Cambridge University Press, London 1955. Reprinted in many textbooks.

[4] Some of the following types of definitions are discussed by Tord Simonsson in his article, 'Der Religiöse Satz', *Neue Zeitschrift für Systematische Theologie und Religionsphilosophie*, IX, 1967, pp.218–27.

A second type of definition is to define a religious sentence as one containing certain words – such as God, Jesus, or Mohammed – or having the same meaning as a sentence containing these words. Such a definition is discussed and refuted by Bernard Williams in his contribution to *New Essays in Philosophical Theology*.[5] A definition which points out a certain technical terminology as being common and peculiar to religious statements seems at least to have the same defects as a definition referring to certain documents.

In the article mentioned, Williams tries to work out a kind of definition which focuses on the subject-matter of religious language. Just as a sentence in mycology might be defined as a sentence about fungi, so a religious sentence might be defined as a sentence about God. Williams says, 'For religious language . . . is, peculiarly, language about God; and by "peculiarly" I mean not only that all religious language is language about God, but – and this seems to me an important point – that all language about God is religious language.'[6] By making three modifications, Williams succeeds in giving his definition a certain plausibility. The first modification is to extend the meaning of 'about God' to apply also to prayers to God, rules for a life in obedience to God, etc. Secondly, when saying that all religious language is about God, Williams restricts the meaning of 'religious' to 'Christian'. The third modification is necessary, according to Williams, if the definition – in combination with the assertion that a religious language exists – is not to have as a consequence that God also exists.[7] Williams seems to mean that, instead of simply 'about God', we should read the definition as 'which according to a religious believer is about

[5] Bernard Williams, 'Tertullian's Paradox,' *New Essays in Philosophical Theology*, ed. Antony Flew and Alasdair MacIntyre, SCM Press, London 1955, p.197.

[6] Op. cit., pp.196f.

[7] On p.198, Williams perhaps disregards the complex use of 'about' in ordinary language. From the fact that there are sentences about ghosts, for example, it does not follow that there are ghosts. For an analysis of 'about' see Nelson Goodman, 'About', *Mind* LXX, 1961, pp.1–24. Cf. also our remarks below on the different localization of statements.

God'. We will not here discuss Williams' arguments in any detail. The important thing from our point of view is that semantic definitions of this type have difficulty in satisfying the requirement of analytical neutrality. By stating, in the stipulative definition, what the sentences are about – or are believed to be about – it is all too easy to anticipate one analysis and exclude another. When Braithwaite, for example, finds, as a result of his analysis, that religious assertions are assertions of an intention to carry out a certain behaviour policy, we can ask whether such an assertion is religious by Williams' definition.[8]

An entirely different type of definition seems to underlie an argument in Bochenski's book, *The Logic of Religion*.[9] Bochenski argues as if a religious sentence can be distinguished from a non-religious sentence with reference to the different types of reason that could be adduced for what is said. Definitions referring to reasons which have been given, or could be given, for what we say in religious sentences obviously resemble more an incipient analysis than any analytically neutral proposal for border-lines for the application of the term 'religious sentence' – not to mention the difficulties that arise in discriminating between religious and non-religious reasons, and between reasons that 'could' or 'could not' be given.

An analysis of religious language based on a definition of any of the types discussed above can, of course, be of great philosophical interest, although the deficiencies of such definitions may cause difficulty. In contrast to the first four kinds, however, the fifth makes the analysis of religious language an affair for religious men only. To this group we assign all definitions based on specific theological assumptions. A clear example is provided by the German theologian Hans Grass, who suggests the following preliminary definition: 'Religious sentences are sentences in which God is addressed in prayer and confession

---

[8] Cf. Blackstone, op. cit., p.39.

[9] Joseph M. Bochenski, *The Logic of Religion*, New York University Press, New York 1965, p.71. This is not a very important point in Bochenski's book. On some fundamental issues we shall come to conclusions which are similar to Bochenski's.

and in which God addresses us with demands and promises.'[10] On the face of it, this bears some resemblance to that of Williams, which is discussed above. The important difference, however, is that, according to Grass, a denial that religion is an illusion is a necessary condition for the assumption that there are religious sentences. From Grass's further arguments it follows that more specific theological problems will be involved in the problem of indicating which religious sentences are real religious sentences. I have found no such clearly stated theological definition of a 'religious sentence' in the English literature on the subject, but we should bear in mind the possibility that a philosopher may have an understood definition of this kind. We want, in this book, to avoid theological premises.

The definition adopted in this book   Another of the many possible kinds of definition is one that characterizes a religious sentence with reference to the situation in which it is uttered. Ian Ramsey's discussion in his *Religious Language* suggests that he has a definition of this kind in mind, although it is never explicitly stated.[11] We shall now formulate such a definition, and try to give it sufficient precision, without coming back to the difficulties illustrated above. Our definition has nothing more in common with that suggested in Ramsey's text than the reference to a certain kind of situation. Let us begin with the following:

RS is a religious sentence = def. RS is connected with a religious situation.

What our definition actually says will depend on what we mean by the two terms 'connected with' and 'religious situation'. For 'religious situation' we would stipulate the following meaning: 'That a situation is religious means that the adherents of a certain religion count it as an exercise of that religion to

---

[10] 'Religiöse Sätze sind Sätze, in denen zu Gott geredet wird in Gebet und Bekenntnis und in denen Gott zu uns redet in Anspruch und Zuspruch': Hans Grass, 'Erwägungen über den religiösen Satz', *Neue Zeitschrift für Systematische Theologie und Religionsphilosophie*, IX, 1967, p.130.

[11] Ian T. Ramsey, *Religious Language*, SCM Press, London 1957, for example p.26. Cf. Richard H. Bell, 'Wittgenstein and Descriptive Theology', *Religious Studies* V, 1969, p.7.

engage in the situation *and* that the adherents of that religion do not find it possible to participate seriously in the situation without exercising religion.'

We must now consider the classical question of how to define religion. I think that William James's remarks on this subject are still relevant: '. . . the very fact that they (the definitions of religion) are so many and so different from one another is enough to prove that the word "religion" cannot stand for any single principle or essence, but is rather a collective name . . . We may very likely find no one essence, but many characters which may alternately be equally important in religion.'[12] James sees clearly that what we generally refer to by the word 'religion' are entities which have precisely the relation to each other that Wittgenstein called family resemblance.[13] For our purpose, it is sufficient to enumerate what we count as religions:[14] Judaism, Christianity, Islam, Hinduism, and Buddhism. The list is adequate, but we could have made it much longer without any consequence to the analysis. If, however, we were to add such theories as Chinese Marxism, then the situation would become complicated. Examples of religious situations according to our definition are praying to God, reading the Apostles' creed in church, walking around the Kaba.

We now have to establish the meaning of 'connected with'. That a sentence is 'connected with' a religious situation means, we shall say:

(*a*) that the uttering of the sentence is part of what constitutes the situation, or

[12] William James, *The Varieties of Religious Experience*, Longmans, Green & Co., London 1903 (first ed. 1902), p.26.

[13] I use the term in the sense specified in the article 'The Concept of Family Resemblance in Wittgenstein's Later Philosophy' by Hjalmar Wennerberg, *Theoria* XXXIII, 1967, pp.107–32. See pp.112f.

[14] For a discussion of the definitions of religion see especially William Christian, *Meaning and Truth in Religion*, Princeton University Press, Princeton 1964, Chapter III. Christian clearly points out the insufficiency of a general definition of religion by enumeration: 'Then we would have no way of recognizing novel forms of religion, although, from the history of religion, we have good reason to expect some to emerge' (pp.35f.).

(*b*) that the sentence says something which is taken for granted by a group of believers when they participate seriously in a religious situation *and* the refutation of which would constitute a good reason for them never seriously to participate in such a religious situation.

Examples of religious sentences according to (*a*) are the hymn text which is part of what constitutes the religious situation of singing a hymn, and the sentence, 'I baptize . . .' By interviewing persons walking around the Kaba, we could obtain a list of sentences that are religious according to (*b*).

The definition now outlined seems to satisfy the ordinary-use requirement. It is also analytically neutral. Nothing is said as to the meaning, reference, or function of religious sentences. But does our definition really make the term more precise? It is obvious that a certain vagueness of the term 'religious sentence' will remain. This is due to the vagueness of such terms as 'adherent of Christianity', etc., which occur in the definiens. This remaining vagueness, however, is not of a kind that will create any difficulty in the analysis. All sentences which may lie on the border-line of the application-area of the term 'religious sentence' will have the same properties as a sentence to which the term obviously applies. For any sentence of analytical importance, the question of whether or not it is religious can be answered, if we adopt this definition, by an ordinary empirical investigation. By our definition, what we call religious sentences are sets of sentence-tokens which it is possible to characterize by reference to the situations in which they are used.

2. *Analytical terminology*

Complaints are often voiced that no generally accepted terms and concepts for the philosophical analysis of language exist – outside logic. The various terminologies are often not susceptible to translation into each other. They are linked by different approaches to the analysis or by different theories of language. We shall here endeavour to employ an analytical terminology which suggests no special theory of language, and which incorporates concepts from different schools. However, the choice of a conceptual apparatus for an analysis means adopting a standpoint on certain controversial questions. Our choice of concepts will be justified if it proves fruitful when used for the analysis. Terminologically, we will try to use, as far as possible, terms already introduced by different schools: unfortunately, however, we must also introduce certain new terms.

Let us begin by indicating four different things we can do in uttering a sentence in natural language.

Statement The first is to assert or state that something is the case. When a sentence is used in this way, we call the sentence a 'statement'.[15] (Only synthetic statements are considered here.)

Expression In uttering a sentence, we can also be expressing an emotive or conative reaction towards something. A sentence so used we call an 'expression'.

Prescription Another type of act which can be performed by uttering a sentence is to prescribe something that should be done. Sentences with which we do this are termed 'prescriptions'.

Performative We sometimes create a new state of affairs by uttering a sentence. When I say 'I promise . . .', then a promise is realized. I am not asserting that something is the case when I am promising, but as a description of what I am doing when I say 'I promise . . .' it is a true statement to say, 'I promise . . .' Certain acts – such as promising – have the following characteristic. When the circumstances are right, then to perform the act it is enough to utter a sentence which is such that it can also be used as a statement describing the act. When we perform

[15] In our terminology we speak of the use of sentences as statements, expressions, etc. We do not in any analogous way say that there is a use of statements, expressions. etc. This terminology is on the same lines as Gilbert Ryle's in his famous discussion of the distinction between 'use' and 'usage' (see *Philosophy and Linguistics*, ed. Colin Lyas, Macmillan, London 1971, especially Chapter II). One can get the opposite impression because he refuses to speak about the use of sentences. His concept of *sentence*, however, is different from ours. Cf. William P. Alston, *Philosophy of Language*, Prentice-Hall, Inc., Englewood Cliffs, N.J. 1964, p.33.

an act in this way, our utterance is a 'performative'.[16] Examples: 'I swear . . .', 'I baptize . . .', 'I guarantee . . .'.

Our classification of utterances into four groups is, of course, a rough one. It by no means does justice to the manifold uses to which sentences are actually put. In the following chapters, we will have to introduce many other distinctions. However, the characteristics which allow us to form the four sets of sentences are of decisive importance in an analysis of religious sentences, and we will therefore take the distinction between statements, expressions, etc., as a starting-point for our investigation. It is necessary also to bear in mind that sentences having the same formal characteristics can be used in such a way as to belong to more than one of these four sets.

A common name for what we are doing when, by uttering a sentence, we assert, express, prescribe, etc., is that we are performing a 'speech-act'. The sentences used as statements, expressions, etc., can be said to have different 'functions'. The function of a sentence which is a statement, for instance, is often called 'informative', but we are not going to use this term. Truth and falsehood are properties only of statements. We could say that statements are theoretical or cognitive from the point of view of logical status.

Anchorage of sentences   The relationship between a speech-act and the state of affairs in the world is very complicated. To discuss this, we would have to investigate how certain words in a sentence 'designate', what is meant when we say that a sentence 'is about' anything, etc. No such investigation is required here. It is sufficient to note that, in performing a speech-act, we generally make a supposition concerning the existence of certain states of affairs. Saying 'Stop the war in Vietnam!' or 'There is a war in Vietnam', we suppose certain things about what is taking place in Vietnam. The state of affairs which is supposed in uttering a sentence will be called the 'anchorage'

---

[16] This definition of performative comes close to Chisholm's definition of 'strict performative'. See Roderick M. Chisholm, *Theory of Knowledge*, Prentice-Hall, Inc., Englewood Cliffs, N. J. 1966, p.16.

of the sentence. The anchorage is a state of affairs, the existence of which is supposed. It is not the supposition of a state of affairs. Often an anchorage which does not exist in the real world[17] is nevertheless supposed to exist in the real world by many persons. To find out what the anchorage of a certain statement, expression, prescription, or performative is we will have to investigate the function of the sentence among speakers and hearers. To find out if the anchorage exists in the real world we would have to investigate the world in general.

The anchorage of a *statement* is called its 'reference'. It is the state of affairs which makes the statement true. If the reference of a statement does not exist, then the statement is false.

If it is possible in principle to find out empirically whether or not the anchorage exists in the real world, then we shall say that we can 'verify empirically' or 'falsify empirically' the existence of the anchorage. If it is empirically verified that the anchorage of a certain statement exists, then we shall say that the statement is 'empirically verified', etc. We need not introduce here any distinction between verification and confirmation, but we will use the term 'verification' in a broad sense also to cover the cases which might in strict terms have been called 'confirmation'. A fundamental thesis of empiricism is *the standpoint that there is no other anchorage for a language in the real world than one which it is possible in principle to verify empirically*. We shall refer to this thesis as 'the minimum thesis of empiricism'. The logical empiricists claimed much more about language, but we need not enter into any discussion concerning the verification-principle, etc.[18] The fundamental problems of religious language to which the logical empiricists drew

[17] When I use the phrase 'real world' I mean it as opposed to 'imagined world' or 'a world of fantasy'. If there is something transcendent, something having characteristics quite different from anything we know by our senses, then according to my terminology this transcendent reality belongs to the real world.

[18] There are many good surveys describing the development of logical empiricism and its view of religion. See for instance, Frederick Ferré, *Language, Logic and God*, Eyre and Spottiswoode, London 1962, Chapters 1–4. Cf. also Blackstone, op. cit., pp.52f.

attention will emerge when this language is confronted with the minimum thesis of empiricism.

Localization   In our everyday speech, we use sentences which are statements, expressions, prescriptions and performatives. But these kinds of speech-acts are also performed by, for instance, an actor playing Hamlet. In the latter case the anchorage of the sentences belongs to a fictitious world. When the anchorage of a sentence belongs to a world which is fictitious or ideal, the sentence will be said to have a different 'localization' from sentences which have an anchorage in the real world. A statement in a drama may be true or false within the drama's own fictitious world. The same statement may sometimes have the same truth-value when located in the real world. This is the situation in certain documentary plays. Usually, a change in a statement's localization will alter its truth-value.[19] Sentences which are performatives in one localization can never at the same time be performatives in another localization. If an actor says in a drama, 'I promise . . .', this is a promise in the world of that drama, but when the play is over the promise no longer exists.[20] In a modern play, however, it is possible that an artist will make a promise on the stage which is a promise even when the curtain goes down. But what he is then doing is to give his utterance another localization than we are used to expecting from a person on stage. He is not uttering a performative in a fictitious world which is also a performative in the real world. In describing the anchorage of an expression uttered by a person in the real world, we sometimes have to use a statement with a

[19] What is here called the anchorage of a statement located in the real world corresponds to the 'denotatum' of a sign in the terminology of Charles Morris. Morris's 'designatum' is analogous to the anchorage of a statement independent of its localization. See Charles W. Morris, *Foundations of the Theory of Signs* (International Encyclopedia of Unified Science, Volumes I and II; Foundations of the Unity of Science, Volume I, Number 2), The University of Chicago Press, Chicago 1938, p.5.

[20] Readers interested in curiosities in the history of ideas may here observe Samuel Pufendorf, *De Jure Naturae et Gentium*, 1672 (The Classics of International Law, 17, ed. James Brown Scott, Clarendon Press, Oxford 1934), Book I, Chapter I, §15.

fictitious localization. Let us, for instance, imagine a person who is convinced that there are no ghosts in the real world. In certain circumstances he may still express a fear of ghosts. The anchorage of the expression is certain describable real states of affairs, and also the presence of ghosts. But to say that there were ghosts present is to make a statement with a fictitious localization. If an expression voices the emotions of a real person in his daily life, and we use a statement with a fictitious localization to describe the anchorage, then the expression will be said to have a 'fictitious localization in a weak sense'.

Indirect statement   A set of sentences located in a fictitious world can together have an important relation to the real world, even if no single statement is true when located in the real world. The fictitious world created by different speech-acts may lead us to find something which is the case in the real world. It may, for instance, lead us to discover a certain psychological fact. Sentences, located in a fictitious world, which can state something true or false about the real world, and which do not say the same thing if seen as located in the real world, will here be called 'indirect statements'.[21]

Indirect expressions and prescriptions   A fictitious world created by different speech-acts may also have the function of expressing emotions, conative impulses or prescriptions which concern the real world. Sartre's drama *Huis clos* may be said not only to express the emotions of certain fictitious persons but, as a whole, to express an emotion with which many of us are familiar and which concerns situations in daily life. Sentences which have their localization in a fictitious world, which can express certain emotions or conative impulses for persons in the real world and which do not express the same reactions if seen as located in the real world, will here be called 'indirect expressions'.

[21] The truth concerning the real world of an indirect statement or – which is the normal case – a set of indirect statements can be what J. Hospers has called *truth to* life as distinct from *truth about* life. The truth of a statement with a localization in the real world always involves *truth about* life. See John Hospers, *Meaning and Truth in the Arts*, University of North Carolina Press, Chapel Hill 1946, pp.162ff.

Analogically, we shall speak of 'indirect prescriptions'. It should be observed that sentences which are statements if located in a certain fictitious world can be indirect expressions when we observe the relation of this fictitious world to the real world. Expressions with a fictitious localization in a weak sense can also express complicated emotional processes concerning the real world. They will also be called indirect expressions. When a sentence is used in a speech-act as an indirect statement, expression, etc., we shall call it an 'indirect sentence'.

Meaning   We have, up to now, avoided the key-term 'meaning'. The reason is that we want to avoid, as far as possible, any general discussion of semantic questions which have little relevance to our further investigation. However, we cannot avoid the term, and we must introduce another stipulative definition. The meaning of a sentence, in our terminology, is that property of the sentence through which it can be a certain statement, a certain expression, a certain prescription or a certain performative. If two sentences in a situation are understood by a person as the same speech-act, then the two sentences have the same meaning for this person in this situation. If when my son comes to the dinner-table, I say 'Please wash your hands!' or 'Your hands are dirty', he may understand the two sentences as the same prescription. They then have the same meaning for him in the particular situation, although the grammatical form of the second is that generally used for statements. Our use of the term 'meaning' is not an adherence to any of the 'theories of meaning', but it is incompatible with those theories that, for instance, equate meaning and reference. The present use of the term 'meaning' is different from that common among the logical empiricists, for instance. Their standpoint may, in our terminology, be expressed by saying that they reserved the term meaning for those sentences which are statements that could be empirically verified or falsified, or which are analytic statements.[22]

---

[22] For a short presentation of the theories of meaning see Alston, op. cit., Chapters 1 and 2.

We have now introduced the term meaning, but we have not presented any analysis of what meaning is. This would mean an excessive excursion from the argument.

Descriptive and constructive investigations An investigation – philosophical or linguistic – of a certain realm of language can take various forms. Let us begin by indicating two kinds of empirical descriptive investigation.

Descriptive 1 In the first kind, the properties of the language used by persons in a certain society or culture are examined and described. What is of interest to us is the properties that can be described in the terminology introduced above. But how can we establish empirically whether or not a certain sentence is, for instance, a statement? The basic method seems to be to study the reactions regularly evoked by the sentence in a community where the sentence is used. Let us suppose A says to B, 'There are a lot of books on my table', and that A says nothing more about the table. If we doubt that A's utterance is a statement, we can see how B reacts to the following questions: (1) 'What do you think is lying on A's table?' (2) 'If you have any idea of what is lying on A's table, where did you get it from?' (3) 'Did A tell you to do anything with the things on his table?' If B's answer is to (1) 'Books', to (2) 'A told me' and to (3) 'No', then we can conclude that B in this situation took A's sentence to be a statement. If he had answered to (3) 'A asked me to take the books', then the sentence would have been taken by B as a prescription in this situation. By investigating what reactions certain sentences in a language normally evoke in certain situations, we could establish on empirical grounds that a given sentence in a given communicative situation is generally a statement, and so on.[23] In some cases we may find

[23] The use of a sentence is often rather homogeneous in a society. This means that the same sentence in the same kind of situation generally is used to perform the same speech-act. If we have reason to assume that this is the case, we need only examine a few instances of a sentence in the same kind of situation in order to establish how the sentence is used in a society. We are then in a position similar to the anatomist's when he investigates the structure of the human body. He is often permitted to generalize his results

out by a questionnaire or otherwise what a particular person *intended* to say by using a particular sentence in a particular situation. Sometimes this will not coincide with the normal use of this sentence in such a situation. If a person, in a given situation, uses a sentence which in this situation is normally a statement to express certain emotions, he may be completely misunderstood, and he will have to declare in some way that he is not using the language in the normal way.

An easier way than the questionnaire method to find out how a sentence is used in a certain situation is to ask people what other sentences would have the same meaning in this situation. If we find that many people would understand A's sentence in our example to have the same meaning as 'Take away the books on my table', then we can conclude that A's sentence in this situation can be a prescription. This conclusion is justified because we already know empirically that in our language a sentence with the form 'Take away the books . . .' is generally a prescription. The fact that there is a large number of sentences which have a clearly established use in a community makes it possible that the difficulty of establishing the use of a problematic sentence can often be overcome by establishing what other sentences can have the same meaning in the situation in question. It is often the case that one and the same sentence, in a certain situation, can be understood in many different ways. In order to single out one as the correct interpretation of the sentence, we must be able to state the criteria of a correct interpretation. For an empirical description of language, it is not necessary to possess such criteria.

Descriptive 2   An entirely different question concerning the use of language can also be answered by an empirical descriptive investigation, namely, 'How do people think they are using

---

on the basis of an examination of a low number of bodies. I think that we are often in this situation when we study the use of sentences as statements, etc. Perhaps G. Ryle has made too much of this simple fact when he works out his distinction between use and usage. See G. Ryle, 'Use and Usage', *Philosophy and Linguistics*, ed. Colin Lyas, p.49.

1957410I

the language?'. Some persons have certain ideas as to how sentences in their language are normally used. These ideas are open to empirical investigation by the same kind of sociological method as indicated above. It is not impossible that a majority of English-speaking persons have an idea which, in our terminology, can be expressed by saying that all declarative sentences are statements. By an empirical investigation of the first kind, we can easily find that this idea is wrong. There is reason to suppose that many people entertain wrong ideas as to the use of their own language.

Constructive From the descriptive study of language we must distinguish the constructive. A constructive study aims to make the language better than it is according to a descriptive investigation. To do this, we must possess certain criteria of the qualities of a language. One such criterion could be this. If use (*a*) of a sentence leads to contradictions with a scientific theory and use (*b*) does not, then use (*b*) is better than use (*a*). Let us say that we can discern two different uses of the sentence 'This lake is beautiful'. The first is to use it as a statement. What is said is that the lake has a certain property, beauty. The second use is to take the sentence as an expression. Certain emotions towards the lake are voiced through the use of the sentence. We could then, for the sake of the example, imagine that the first use is the more common, but that no such properties as beauty exist. A constructive theory may now claim that the second use is the correct one.

Explanatory theories A third main kind of approach is to try to provide an explanation of the function which a sentence has according to a descriptive theory, or ought to have according to a constructive one. Theories which are the result of such a study we shall call 'explanatory' theories. The correctness or otherwise of these theories must be tested empirically. In the field of language this is often difficult in practice, and explanatory theories are consequently sometimes rather unreliable.

A
200. I

II

RELIGIOUS STATEMENTS

Introduction In this chapter we shall investigate the literature on religious statements. This is a battlefield on which nearly all modern English-speaking philosophers of religion have been involved, in some small skirmish or other. Most textbooks in the philosophy of religion contain a survey of this field. If anyone were to count the times John Wisdom's and Antony Flew's parable of the gardener – which illustrates the problem of religious statements – has been retold, he would reach a surprisingly high figure.[1]

Theories of religious statements are generally divided into two main classes.[2] According to the first class of theories – called cognitive, propositional, etc. – there are certain impor-

[1] The parable first appears in Wisdom's well-known essay 'Gods', *Proceedings of the Aristotelian Society*, N.S. XLV, 1944–45, pp.185–206. The essay has been reprinted many times. See Wisdom's *Philosophy and Psychoanalysis*, Basil Blackwell, Oxford 1953. Flew's version is found in *New Essays in Philosophical Theology*. As stated by James Richmond in his *Theology and Metaphysics*, SCM Press, London 1970, pp.63ff., the parable is much more discussed in Flew's version than in Wisdom's. The differences, however, are important. See further Richmond, op. cit., pp.64ff. It is a correct observation that Wisdom uses the parable in a way which is more favourable to theology. However, it is necessary to keep in mind what Renford Bambrough says in his *Reason, Truth and God*, Methuen, London 1969, p.91. 'Wisdom's account promises reassurance to the theologian, and performs at least part of what it promises. . . . But I have suggested that the reassurance is not permanent and stable. At the end of this road there arises another barrier, the barrier of divine transcendence' (Bambrough uses many arguments which are similar to Wisdom's).

[2] See, for instance, Reaburne S. Heimbeck, *Theology and Meaning*, George Allen and Unwin, London 1969, pp.21f.; J. M. Bochenski, *The Logic of Religion*, p.40.

tant religious sentences which are statements. This is denied
by the second class of theories, which are often called non-
cognitive. This dichotomy points out an important tendency
in the debate, but it is far too rough a classification for the
purpose of analysing the arguments for and against these
theories. We shall here proceed to formulate five questions
which are important for the analysis of those religious sentences
which might be statements. In finding what answers are given
by the existing theories, we shall see how they can be interpreted, what arguments are adduced for the different standpoints, and what kinds of argument are relevant. We also hope
that a discussion of these questions will lead us to the formulation
of new subjects of research into the role of statements in
religious language, and to adequate methods for that research.

1. 'The problematic set of religious sentences'

Definition   One set of religious sentences is of central importance
to the discussion of religious statements. This is *the set of religious
sentences which have the linguistic shape generally used for statements,
and which will remain when we have removed those religious sentences
which are used as empirically testable statements by religious believers.*
We shall call this set 'the problematic set of religious sentences'.

Examples   For a modern educated Christian man, the following
sentences can probably be placed in the problematic set: 'God
created the world.' 'An angel visited the Virgin Mary.' 'Christ
was dead but arose again from the dead after three days.'[3]
Sentences which are religious by our definition but do not
belong to the problematic set include, for example: 'Mohammed moved from Mecca to Medina in the year 622.' 'Jesus was
crucified near Jerusalem.' 'The children of Israel emigrated
from Egypt under the leadership of Moses.'

As we shall see, many theories can be interpreted as applicable

---

[3] Ninian Smart in his *Reasons and Faiths*, pp.21ff., explains 'why propositions about Brahman are not simple empirical ones'. In doing that he shows
how many important religious sentences in Indian religion must belong to
the problematic set of religious sentences.

to the problematic set of sentences. Some writers, however, deny the possibility of dividing up religious sentences as we have done, by defining the problematic set of sentences. This kind of theory will be discussed in connection with our last question.

We can now proceed to the first of our questions.

2. *Are any religious sentences members of the problematic set?*

Theories referring fundamental religious sentences to the problematic set interpreted as descriptive 1   One point in the application of the parable of the gardener by Flew and many others is the theory which states that an increasing number of religious sentences are referred to the problematic set when religious men are confronted with science. As a result, the fundamental religious sentences belong, according to this theory, to the problematic set. The advocates of such a theory believe that many religious sentences begin their history as empirical hypotheses and, as such, do not belong to the problematic set. When religious men are confronted with empirical data and scientific theories which threaten to falsify a religious hypothesis, then they start to deny that empirical data have any bearing upon the hypothesis, and the sentence is referred to the problematic set of sentences. Which kind of theory is this? Flew and many others express themselves as if part of it were a descriptive theory.[4] They pretend to say something true of religious language as used by religious men. We shall first interpret the theory as descriptive.

Opposing theories interpreted as descriptive 1   Of course, Flew's answer to our first question is opposed by many writers. Such opposing theories may also be interpreted as descriptive. Let us take Reaburne S. Heimbeck as a fair representative. Heimbeck's theories of religious language are not only descriptive,[5] but just as part of Flew's theory can be seen as a theory about the use of religious language among religious men, so too can

---

[4] See *New Essays in Philosophical Theology*, p.98, and Braithwaite, op. cit., pp.6f.

[5] Heimbeck, *Theology and Meaning*, p.35.

part of Heimbeck's answer to Flew be interpreted as a descriptive theory.

Heimbeck does not say that there are no religious sentences which belong to the problematic set. He expressly limits himself to the traditional Christian language and to sentences containing the word 'God' (G-sentences in Heimbeck's terminology), but his examples of sentences are precisely those which are referred to the problematic set by Flew's and similar theories. There are at least some religious sentences the analysis of which is contradictory in the theories represented by Flew and Heimbeck. Heimbeck's argument is that many of the religious sentences that are in Flew's theory members of the problematic set entail other sentences which are ordinary empirical statements open at least to empirical falsification. This means that such religious sentences are testable in the same manner as, for instance, sentences about electric current (Heimbeck's example) and do not belong to the problematic set. Heimbeck chooses as an example the sentence: 'God has provided all men, through the life, death, and resurrection of Jesus of Nazareth, the grace sufficient for eternal salvation.' This sentence, he argues, entails: 'Jesus of Nazareth was alive at t_1, dead both clinically and biologically at t_2, and alive again in bodily form at t_3.'[6] The last sentence is obviously a statement that is empirically falsifiable. It follows that the first one can also be falsified. It does not belong to what we have called the problematic set of sentences. Heimbeck takes for granted that the semantical entailment-relation holds between the two sentences in the example. This is a descriptive hypothesis about the use of language among religious men.[7]

Method of determining which of the theories is correct   What method,

[6] Heimbeck, op. cit., p.95. A similar argument is found in Thomas McPherson, *The Philosophy of Religion*, Van Nostrand, London 1965, pp.194ff. However, McPherson has a somewhat different view on the relation which Heimbeck calls 'entailment'. Our account of Heimbeck's book in this chapter does not do justice to his main point about patterns of evidence and G-configurations. These last theories can be interpreted in such a way that they have some analogies to our thesis in Chapter V.

[7] This noted by Heimbeck, for instance on p.177.

then, can be used to determine which of the two conflicting answers to our first question is correct? We have interpreted the two theories as descriptive. It is consequently obvious that the adequate method is an ordinary empirical investigation. First we have to choose a group of religious men, who can be taken as representative of a larger group according to ordinary statistical methods. Following our definition in Chapter I, we can find out what sentences are religious for these men. From these religious sentences we must then try to make a representative collection of those which have the form generally used for statements. Our task will be to establish through some kind of sociological testing which of these sentences are used by religious men as statements that can in principle be demonstrated as true by empirical science. We must also find for which of the sentences these religious men can imagine certain empirical facts, the existence of which would be a sufficient condition for refusing to accept the sentence as a part of their religious language. This latter can hardly be achieved by a straightforward interview. We might use questions of the following kind: 'Imagine a person who claims to believe both that Jesus is the Son of God and that Joseph was his biological father. Do you think that such a person contradicts himself?' By means of similar questioning we might test whether the entailment-relations presupposed by Heimbeck really held in religious language. To design a method for this kind of sociological research would be difficult, but not impossible.

One argument against the relevance of empirical research refuted   One argument put forward by Heimbeck against Basil Mitchell can be interpreted as an argument against the relevance of any sociological test to our question. Mitchell's reasoning is similar to Heimbeck's.[8] He discusses the sentence 'God loves all human beings' – one of the main candidates for the problematic set – and says that events in the empirical world count against it, but not (and here he diverges from Heimbeck) conclusively.

[8] Basil Mitchell, 'Theology and Falsification', in *New Essays in Philosophical Theology*, p.105.

For the believer, he says, 'is committed by his faith to trust in God'. Heimbeck replies: 'Religious commitment may account for a believer's not *regarding* anything as counting conclusively against his belief, but this has little or nothing to do with the question of whether or not there are rules (procedures) which determine under what circumstances a G-statement *must be regarded* as conclusively falsified. . .'.[9] Heimbeck's argument is here in error. Logical and scientific rules and the result of their application are surely independent of religious men and their use of the rules; in order, however, to apply the rules to what is said in a sentence, we must know how the sentence is to be interpreted. This is precisely the question to which we shall obtain one kind of answer by an empirical test. We can find out what interpretation is common among religious men. To state the entailments, as Heimbeck does and as we have given as an example, is not to apply a logical rule or to state a scientific fact: it is a part of the interpretation of a religious sentence. Heimbeck admits this himself when he introduces the term 'entailment': '. . . under the semantical account of entailment, p entails q if and only if the truth of p necessitates the truth of q expressly because the meaning of the sentence used to make p includes the meaning of the sentence used to make q, and not by virtue of the syntactical forms of the sentences used in making p and q.'[10]

The importance of analytical neutrality in the definition of religious sentences Comparing the arguments put forward by the philosophers for their various answers to our first question, we find that none of them has made any attempt at empirical research. They refer only to their personal impressions of how religious men use the language, and it is far from certain that different philosophers have the same group of religious men in mind, or that their definitions of the sentences analysed are analytically neutral. Heimbeck discusses, as we have seen, sentences containing the word 'God' (G-sentences). But he makes two restrictions. First, he states that his discussion is limited to 'religious'

[9] Heimbeck, op. cit., p.101.   [10] Heimbeck, op. cit., p.52.

G-sentences, and, secondly, he says that he only wants to analyse G-sentences in 'the classical Christian tradition'.[11] He gives no definition of 'religious' or 'classical Christian tradition', but expressly excludes many modern theologians from the view of religious language he discusses. This means that if we find empirically that many sentences containing the word 'God' belong to the problematic set, Heimbeck could answer that they are not religious or do not belong to the classical Christian tradition. His definition thus runs the risk of not being analytically neutral.

A way to further knowledge   If we take our first question as one that can be answered by empirical research and accept definitions of the kind introduced in Chapter I, we could formulate many interesting hypotheses which could be tested to give us a further knowledge of the religions.

A few examples of such hypotheses:

 (i)   In the language of nearly all religious men, some sentences belong to the problematic set.

 (ii) Owing to the doctrine of the Incarnation, fewer sentences belong to the problematic set in the Christian language than in the Buddhist language. (Christianity is thus more open to empirical falsification.)

 (iii) Educated men of all religions use religious language in such a way that more sentences belong to the problematic set than is the case with the language used by persons knowing nothing of scientific method.

Descriptive theories 2   We have now discussed theories relating to the factual use of religious sentences, i.e. descriptive theories of the first type (p.17). It may be that religious men who are not theologians or philosophers entertain common beliefs about their own use of religious sentences as ordinary statements and as sentences belonging to the problematic set. If this is the case, we can discuss these beliefs and obtain a descriptive theory of the second type (p.18). I do not, however, think that such sophisticated metatheories exist among ordinary religious

[11] Heimbeck, op. cit., p.40 n.2 and p.43.

men, and we need not here consider descriptive theories of this type.

Theories referring fundamental religious sentences to the problematic set interpreted as constructive We shall now ask if any of the answers given to our question might be constructive theories.

Flew's theory of the unfalsifiability of religious sentences could perhaps be interpreted as containing a constructive aspect. When Flew refers certain sentences to the problematic set, he is perhaps saying not only that religious men use the sentences in a way which makes it impossible to falsify what is said, but also that they *ought* to use them in this way, if they are to avoid saying something obviously false. The use of certain religious sentences as members of the problematic set is thus a suggestion which Flew makes in order to discuss whether or not it is reasonable.[12] He then proceeds to find that it is not.

There are, however, some theories according to which it is extremely important, religiously and philosophically, to interpret religious language in such a way as to obtain a positive answer to our first question. This is the kind of constructive theory of which we have a clear example in the theology of Rudolf Bultmann.

An example of such a theory Bultmann proceeds from the assumption that religious men, including the New Testament writers, often use sentences about God as primitive scientific hypotheses. This use of religious sentences results in a 'mythology'. According to Bultmann, sentences about God which are seen as scientific statements can easily be shown to be false.[13] So far his theory is descriptive. The thesis of a mythological use of religious sentences could be tested empirically, and the same applies to the thesis that such mythological statements are false. Bultmann, however, thinks it possible to suggest a better use

[12] Cf. T. R. Miles, *Religion and the Scientific Outlook*, George Allen and Unwin, London 1959, p.139.

[13] A good introduction to Bultmann's mature thought is given in his American lectures of 1951 published under the title *Jesus Christ and Mythology*, SCM Press, London 1960.

of talk about God than the mythological one. In making this correction of religious language, Bultmann refers certain key-sentences to the problematic set. His argument is stated very clearly in a short article from 1925, 'What Does it Mean to Speak of God?'[14]

The first premise of his argument is the theory that there is a certain necessary condition to be fulfilled in order to make true and false statements of a kind that does not belong to the problematic set. His second premise is that this condition is never fulfilled when we speak about God. He then comes to the conclusion that sentences which pretend to say anything about God belong to the problematic set. Bultmann seems to mean that a Christian man is bound to accept these premises. If the Christian then wants to follow ordinary logic, he must correct the traditional understanding of his language and accept the conclusions. Let us look at these premises a little more carefully. The necessary condition for making true or false statements which can be verified or falsified ('Reden über, Reden von, in wissenschaftlichen Sätzen reden') is, according to Bultmann, that we should be able to take a point of view ('Standpunkt') outside what we are talking about. It is not clear what this means. There are many senses of 'taking a point of view outside' in which this is not a necessary condition for verifying a statement. I cannot take a point of view outside mankind, but I can make many true statements about mankind. Perhaps we will come closer to Bultmann's point if we say 'be an observer of' instead of 'take a point of view outside'. I can be an observer of myself and of my own emotions, but when I am screaming with pain, my scream is not the result of my being an observer of certain processes in my body. Let us say that my linguistic behaviour in this case has as a necessary condition that I am a participant. It seems true that we must be able to be observers in order to verify or falsify a statement. But it is also true that we can be both observers and participants of the same processes. At the same time that I am screaming with pain

[14] English translation in Rudolf Bultmann, *Faith and Understanding*, SCM Press, London 1969, pp.53–65.

I can verify statements about physiological processes in my body.

The second premise now says that it is impossible to take a point of view outside God, or, as we said above, to be in the position of an observer towards God. For the argument to be conclusive, this must mean not only that the most important relation to God is other than the observer's, but that we can *never* be in the observer's relation to God. This is another situation than suggested in the example with the sensation of pain above. Bultmann compares our relation to God with our relation to our own *Existens*. We shall return to this point. What is now of importance is that his second premise is a religious sentence.[15] Bultmann must be of the opinion that this religious sentence is more important or is better known as true than statements about God which do not belong to the problematic set. His arguments for this opinion are to be found among his reasons for his existentialist base-position and we shall not comment upon them here. Bultmann also believes that the sentences about God which he refers to the problematic set have an important meaning and function. This view will be discussed below.

Summary of the arguments for the theory, and the criteria of their truth
We can now sum up the kind of reasons that are given for this constructive theory which refers certain key-sentences in a religious language to the problematic set. The theory draws attention to one religious statement, which it is supposed to be impossible to abandon. It then shows this sentence to have consequences which necessitate a correction of the common use of the religious language in question. To establish whether or not the argument is correct, we need at least some religious criteria.

[15] An argument similar to Bultmann's is discussed and criticized by William A. Christian, *Meaning and Truth in Religion*, p.253 – point (*d*) – and pp.256ff. Christian does not take up Bultmann but mentions Tillich.

3. Are any sentences belonging to the problematic set of religious sentences statements with their localization in the real world?

The possibility of answering this question by means of a descriptive theory 1   Some of the most widely discussed theories of religious language contain an answer to this question. These are the theories of Flew and other so called non-cognitivists. Their theories are constructive in the parts which contain an answer to our second question. Before discussing these, let us ask if there are any descriptive theories which answer the second question. I have not read of any theories which allow such an interpretation. However, it is an interesting empirical question whether or not religious men in fact use sentences of the problematic set as statements about the real world. A hypothesis which seems probable to me is that they often do. Many people refer, for instance, the sentence 'Jesus is the Son of God' to the problematic set and want, at the same time, to state by the sentence something which is the case in the real world. In communication between Christian persons, sentences of the problematic set, such as 'Jesus is the Son of God', sometimes seem to be used in the same way as ordinary statements such as 'Jesus was born in Bethlehem'.

Descriptive theories 2 and the possibility of their use in a further argument   If we make a descriptive investigation of the second type (p.18), asking how religious men *think* they are using such sentences as we might refer to the problematic set, we will be very likely to find that a great majority think they are using them as statements.[16] Is it possible to draw any further conclusions from this fact? Bochenski presents an argument which, if correct, would allow us to do so. He discusses whether or not religious language contains any statements at all. (In Bochenski's terminology: whether some part of religious discourse [RD]

[16] Cf. Kai Nielsen, 'On Fixing the Reference Range of "God" ', *Religious Studies* 2, 1966, p.14. Observe that from the fact that religious men think that they use a certain sentence as a statement it does not follow that they think that they use the sentence as an *empirically testable* statement.

expresses propositions.) It is evident, according to Bochenski, that religious men *intend* to make statements or *think that* they do so. He then concludes that philosophers who deny the existence of statements in religious language are not offering any analysis of the factual, existing RD, but rather suggesting a completely new sort of RD.[17] William L. Rowe remarks in a review that it does not follow from the fact that someone thinks that in uttering a sentence he is making a statement, that he is really doing so.[18]

If we transform the arguments to our own, more narrow question, an argument analogous to Bochenski's would lead to the conclusion that the analysis of religious language shows that there are in the Christian language direct statements with localization in the real world and that some of these statements belong to the problematic set. Another standpoint would be the suggestion of a new religious language. A philosopher like Rowe would deny the conclusion.

As we have seen, we are not permitted to draw any conclusions as to the use from anyone's belief about the use. If Rowe intends to say this against Bochenski, he is quite right; Rowe is also right if he wants to say that Bochenski over-simplifies the relation between a descriptive theory of either of the two categories and a constructive one. It is a legitimate and natural analytic question to ask if it is possible, according to some philosophical standards, to use the language as religious men do or think they do. It cannot be disregarded by reference to a descriptive theory of category 2. But if the factual use of sentences and the general belief as to that use coincide, which is probably the case in regard to our question, a philosopher, of course, needs strong reason to conclude that this use of language is impossible and must be corrected if we are to continue to use the language. Most theories answering our question in the negative are attempts to give such reasons. They are, as said above, constructive. To refuse to call such a theory an analysis,

17 Bochenski, op. cit., p.42.
18 William L. Rowe, Review of J. Bochenski, *The Logic of Religion*, *Philosophical Review* LXXVI, 1967, p.534.

as Bochenski does, seems pointless. We will now discuss the constructive theories.

Constructive theories denying that sentences belonging to the problematic set can be statements with a localization in the real world   The main argument against accepting any sentence of the problematic set as a statement with localization in the real world is a very simple one. It consists of making certain conditions for a sentence being a statement and then demonstrating that a member of the problematic set of religious sentences cannot satisfy these conditions. The distinction drawn here between different localizations of statements is not explicit in the theories generally discussed. In regard to propositions or statements, however, the philosophers who use the argument mean, in most contexts, statements with localization in the real world. In our terminology the argument can be schematically formulated as follows:

The main argument

(i)   A necessary condition for a sentence being a statement is that there should be a method by which one can determine in principle whether or not the anchorage of the sentence exists in the real world.

(ii)   The only possible methods for determining whether or not anything exists in the real world are $M_1 - M_n$.

(iii)   There is no possible method by which we could determine whether or not an anchorage of any member of the problematic set of religious sentences exists in the real world (from an interpretation of (i) and the definition of the problematic set).

(iv)   The problematic set of religious sentences contains no statements which have localization in the real world (from (i) and (iii)).[19]

[19] We list some examples of books in philosophy of religion which more or less clearly subscribe to the argument:

Antony Flew, *God and Philosophy*. (It seems to emerge from p.22, that an argument similar to the one spelled out here determines Flew's position.)

Ronald W. Hepburn, *Christianity and Paradox*, Watts, London 1958. (See his starting-point on p.18 and his conclusion on p.186.)

The philosophers who use this argument generally state (i) and (ii) together. This is true of Braithwaite, Flew, Hepburn, Nielsen and many others, However, it seems practical to make the division, because a great part of the discussion could be interpreted as concentrating upon (ii), while (i) is seldom disputed. To deny (i) would be to take an irrationalistic point of view.[20]

The argument is presented in an empiricist tradition and its adherents generally accept the minimum thesis of empiricism (p.14). As a typical example of the form taken by (i) and (ii) in the literature, we will quote Kai Nielsen, who says (referring to Flew): 'Religious statements purporting to make factual assertions must be confirmable or disconfirmable in principle by non-religious, straightforwardly empirical, factual statements.'[21] The minimum thesis of empiricism is an interpretation of (ii) which gives (iv) as a conclusion. Those who use the argument also assume as a true descriptive or constructive theory that many important religious sentences belong to the problematic set. Their conclusion, therefore, is that a central area of religious language cannot be said to consist of statements about the real world. A religious man who believes otherwise is seen as in need of correction by a lesson in good philosophy.

The method of establishing whether or not the argument is correct
Many philosophers of religion who argue against this conclusion have stressed the fact that logical empiricism and the

---

T. R. Miles, *Religion and the Scientific Outlook*, p.137. (To indicate an M. for a religious God-sentence would provide the beginning of a solution of the problems which Miles formulates: 'Which is the right frame of reference for the phrase "There is a God", or to what list does the word "God" belong?'. See p.144).

William T. Blackstone, *The Problem of Religious Knowledge*, esp. p.168. (Cf. what Blackstone says here and our argument in Chapter V.)

[20] The theological importance of finding an M and another M than the verification principle in its strict empirical form is stressed in an article by David Cox, 'The Significance of Christianity', *Mind* LIX, 1950, pp.209–18.

[21] Kai Nielsen, 'On fixing the Reference Range of "God" ', *Religious Studies 2*, 1966, p.15.

verification principle of meaning have been sharply criticized in modern linguistic philosophy. They seem to mean that an argument such as Flew's, which follows our scheme, is the result of certain dogmas of logical empiricism that are nowadays generally known to be false.[22] But the criticism of logical empiricism voiced by Wittgenstein and others in no way affects the argument in the form given there.[23] Anyone rejecting it must present another method than the empirical one by which we can gain knowledge of the real world, and then demonstrate by this method that the religious sentences of the problematic set have or lack an anchorage in the real world. Many theories in modern philosophy of religion are, in fact, attempts to find such epistemic theories as will make it possible that premise (ii) and the definition of the problematic set of religious sentences do not give (iii) as a consequence. Perhaps they should be seen as attempts to give a philosophical formulation to the unclear theories existing among those persons of whom it is descriptively true to say that they use the sentences of the problematic set as statements. This means that in order to establish whether or not some of the most discussed theories of religious language answering our second question are correct, we must go back to epistemology. How, then, can we know which epistemological theory is correct? To touch bottom with the criteria of meta-theories of religious language we need a survey of the possible epistemological alternatives to the minimum thesis of empiricism, together with a discussion of the choice between these theories. This will be our task in the last chapter.

[22] See, for example, John A. Hutchinson, *Language and Faith*, The Westminster Press, Philadelphia 1963, pp. 11f.

[23] Cf. Blackstone, op. cit., p.54 and J. Richmond, *Theology and Metaphysics*, p.41. R. W. Hepburn says: 'Within traditional Christian theology questions about the divine existence cannot be deflected into the question "Does God', *Mind* LXXII, 1963, p.41 – Even McKinnon in his interesting parallels between the use of some basic scientific sentences and religious ones escapes too easily – according to my view – the argument on p.32. (Alastair McKinnon, *Falsification and Belief*, Mouton, The Hague 1970.)

4. Are some religious sentences in the problematic set direct statements with a localization other than the real world?

The philosophers who argue against accepting any members of the problematic set of religious sentences as statements do not usually discuss whether such sentences might not have another localization than the real world.[24] If they do, then it is possible to see them as true or false statements, a view which seems, as noted above, to be in accordance with the opinion of most religious men and still to comply with the main argument of the empirical non-cognitivists. By restricting the discussion to statements with one localization, many philosophers may have missed certain important traits of religious language.

A descriptive answer – changing localization among Christians   Let us first discuss what we can say descriptively in regard to this question. In the Christian religious tradition, the narrative of the star of Bethlehem and the wise men who followed it has a very strong position. If someone were to say: 'The star led them not to Bethlehem but to Nazareth', then all Christians would say that the statement was false. The truth, they would agree, is 'The star led the wise men to Bethlehem'. But what, according to the believers, is the localization of this statement? Many, no doubt, would localize it in the real world, imagining that the sentence states a historical fact. A great number of Christians, however, would think that the statement belongs to a fictitious world created by the imagination of the early Christians, influenced as they probably were by similar stories in the Near Eastern tradition. Since Christians of both categories use the same sentences, seeing them as true statements, one might well, in the case of a sermon on the Epiphany, be uncertain as to the localization of such statements. It can be

---

[24] Among the exceptions is, of course, Braithwaite, but he takes up only one aspect of the complex (see below). Interesting remarks concerning the fictitious to be compared with our discussion in section 5 below can be found in I. M. Crombie, 'The Possibility of Theological Statements', *Faith and Logic*, ed. Basil Mitchell, George Allen and Unwin, London 1957, pp. 31–83.

confirmed by empirical research that two Christians can agree as to the truth of a religious statement, but disagree as to its localization. This kind of agreement and disagreement is too seldom indicated.[25]

Biblical examples of changing localization   Uncertainty as to the localization of certain statements and narratives seems to have characterized the biblical religious tradition from the beginning. To take an example from the Old Testament, we can quote the story of the crossing of the Red Sea. According to many exegetes, this narrative was used in the cultus originally as a fictitious story which partakers in the cultus took to express a deep religious truth. Gradually, however, it came to be localized in the real world, and was seen as a description of a specific historical event.[26] Other theories explain the change of localization in a different way, saying for example that the narrative originally had a localization in the real world, and afterwards acquired to some extent a fictitious localization when used as a myth in the cultus. We could take from the New Testament many examples of narratives and details of narratives which have a different localization at different stages of the early tradition. Let us take as an example from recent research the hypothesis that the narratives of the temptation of Jesus in Matt. 4.1–11 had a clearly fictitious localization when they were formulated, in spite of the fact that they seem, on the face of it, to have an obvious localization in the real world as they emerge both in this and the parallel passage. The argument is

[25] An interesting observation of an analogous fluctuation in the use of Christian religious sentences is noted by Kai Nielsen in his article 'On Fixing the Reference Range of "God" ', *Religious Studies 2*, 1966, p.24. Uncertainty as to the localization of Quranic religious sentences can be observed in certain liberal circles of modern Muslims, as is indicated by the following quotation from a Muslim newspaper from Cairo 1941: 'The stories told in the Quran about men of the past are intended for warning and example, not as biography, history, or entertainment . . .' Quoted from H. A. R. Gibb, *Modern Trends in Islam*, University of Chicago Press, Chicago 1947, p.74.
[26] See J. Pedersen, *Israel, Its Life and Culture*. III–IV, Oxford University Press & Branner og Korch, London & Copenhagen 1940, Additional Note I, pp.728–37.

that it can be shown in detail how the narrative has developed as a *haggadic midrash* to Deut. 6–8.[27] (A *haggadic midrash* is a kind of interpretation of the Scriptures used by the Rabbis. It is characterized by the use of a story or parable which illustrates and develops the religious or ethical meaning of the text.)

Disregard of localization and the opposite tendency To a certain extent, the Christian language seems to function without the question of its localization being raised. Many books in systematic theology specify doctrines and draw conclusions without discussing the question.

However, we can notice that Christian believers sometimes find it necessary to give their statements a specific localization. When Saint Paul says: 'If Christ has not been raised, then our preaching is in vain, and your faith is in vain' (I Cor. 15.14), he undoubtedly means that the resurrection has taken place in our real world. It would be worthwhile to investigate what linguistic traits in the text demarcate the localization in such a case.

The descriptive observations summarized and applied to sentences of the problematic set Having made these general reflections, let us restrict ourselves to the problematic set of Christian sentences. It is in these sentences that the three traits we noted above seem to stand out most clearly:

(i) Different Christians accepting the sentences give them a different localization. E.g.: Death came into the world through the first Adam.

(ii) The sentences are sometimes used without any interest in the question of their localization. E.g.: The narrative of the Last Judgment, when quoted nowadays to stress the social responsibility of Christians.

(iii) At least one of the sentences is seen as a statement with localization in the real world. This is the statement 'God

27. See Birger Gerhardsson, *The Testing of God's Son*, Coniectanea Biblica, NT Series 2:1, C. W. K. Gleerup, Lund 1966.

exists' in one of its many Christian interpretations. Most Christians, following Saint Paul, also localize a statement about the resurrection in the real world.

What has now been said is an empirical hypothesis. To work out how these three traits emerge in the Christian language of a certain group of people would need empirical research of a kind which no one has yet attempted.

As regards the situation in other religions, it is difficult even to formulate a hypothesis. In certain forms of Hinduism, we may perhaps find close parallels to Christian language. In Zen Buddhism we might find a tendency to take all sentences of the problematic set as statements having a fictitious localization. An example from an Islamic writer will be discussed in section 5 below.

Comments on a well-known theory interpreted as descriptive   At this point we can consider an aspect of Braithwaite's theory of Christian language. As already indicated, Braithwaite thinks that many sentences in the Christian language belong to the problematic set and that they cannot be statements with a localization in the real world. In a way, however, he regards them as statements. They consistute what he calls a 'story' – i.e. a fictitious narrative like that of *Pilgrim's Progress*. This is the same as saying that they are statements with their localization in a fictitious world. If our hypotheses are correct, then Braithwaite has seen here an important function which such sentences actually possess. But if we take Braithwaite as stating only a descriptive theory, then we must say that he is wrong. He has noticed trait (ii), but not (i) and (iii). Trait (iii) – that at least one sentence of the problematic set is localized in the real world – is incompatible with Braithwaite's theory. This makes it more natural to see Braithwaite's essay as containing a constructive theory which answers the question in the heading of this section – a constructive theory based upon a trait in the factual use of religious language.

Constructive answers   As a constructive theory, the part of Braithwaite's theory here considered is reasonable, if we accept the parts of it that answer the two questions in the titles to sections 2 and 3 of the present chapter. Braithwaite's answer to the first question (section 2) is that many important religious sentences, as a matter of fact, belong to the problematic set. He accepts the minimum thesis of empiricism, and his answer to the second question (section 3) is, therefore, as we have seen above, that these religious sentences cannot reasonably be used as statements with a localization in the real world. Braithwaite, then, has correctly seen the changing localization of religious sentences, and has suggested the utterance of the sentences with another localization than the real world as a reasonable use – i.e. as building up a story. An important point in Braithwaite's theory concerns the meaning of the story. This will be discussed below.

A parallel to Braithwaite's 'stories' are Bultmann's 'myths'. Bultmann has also noticed the changing localization of Christian statements. We have seen that Bultmann – for theological reasons – refers all religious sentences about God to the problematic set and does not see them as statements with a localization in the real world. Bultmann, however, thinks that many sentences which seem to be straightforward statements about the acts of God must be used in religious language. He obviously believes that we must go on speaking about God. When saying this and when denying that the sentences can be statements located in the real world, Bultmann seems to think of them as statements with their localization in a fictitious world. To see this is to see that they constitute, in Bultmann's terminology, a myth. As we shall see below, the function of Bultmann's 'myth' is different from the function of Braithwaite's stories; the similarity is that both the theory of myths and the theory of stories are a development of factual properties of religious sentences, i.e. that they can be used as statements with another localization than the real world, and that their localization is not always definitely fixed in the religious text.

5. *Does the problematic set of religious sentences contain any indirect statements?*

The discussion concerns untranslatable indirect statements As we have seen, there are reasonable descriptive and constructive theories according to which many sentences of the problematic set have another localization than the real world.

A statement with its localization in a fictitious world can have a relation to the real world. It can express emotions towards something in the real world, but it can also indirectly state something in the real world.

Many religious texts can be interpreted as expressing emotions, etc., through sentences which are statements with a fictitious localization.[28] This is the case, for instance, in the psalms. We shall not investigate here the linguistic mechanism which allows us to express emotions and conative impulses by uttering statements with a fictitious localization. Neither shall we discuss the fact that statements with a fictitious localization – probably also religious – can state indirectly an ordinary empirical fact. We shall discuss only such indirect religious sentences as cannot be translated into ordinary empirical statements.

We must first observe a way of interpreting statements with a fictitious localization which is very common in factual religious language.

In popular religious textbooks, the indirect character of some statements is indicated and the indirect statements are translated into sentences which are used as direct statements with a localization in the real world. These sentences are then such that they can be placed among candidates for the problematic set. An example is the narrative of the Creation. It is often denied that the statements contained in Genesis 1 are historically true. Their localization is said to be fictitious. Ac-

---

[28] Cf. N. H. G. Robinson, 'The Logic of Religious Language', in *Talk of God*, Royal Institute of Philosophy Lectures, Vol. II, 1967/8, Macmillan, London 1969, p.5.

cording to Christians, however, Genesis 1 states something true about the real world. This truth could be expressed as follows: 'Everything that exists in the empirical universe is created by God.' This last sentence is a translation of the indirect statements into a sentence which is seen as a direct statement with its localization in the real world. As we can see, the sentence is a possible candidate for membership of the problematic set. The fact that some sentences in the problematic set are used as indirect statements, and that it is possible according to the believers to translate these statements into direct statements with a localization in the real world, is an observation worth noting, but it has little importance from a philosophical point of view if the translation results in sentences of the problematic set.

If, however, we could confirm that there are some indirect statements in a religious language which cannot be translated into direct statements, then this could have important consequences.

A positive descriptive answer and how to find it It is not immediately clear how knowledge-claims of this kind should be met. Perhaps the arguments exluding statements of the problematic kind from a reasonable use of language must be modified, if religious language contains such special kinds of problematic sentences. But how can we proceed to find out if some sentences are used as untranslatable indirect statements? One way is to ask religious people about the truth of their religious statements. We might then find in the Christian tradition that some statements are said not to be true 'in the ordinary way' or 'literally true', but that they are still held to be saying something true. Among these sentences we might easily recognize some indirect statements. We could then ask what is stated in respect of the real world through these statements, and we might receive the answer that this is something impossible to explain. Religious men might also refuse to recognize an ordinary empirical testing procedure for these statements. Investigations of this kind are never performed, but we can guess that the following biblical narratives are accepted by many Christians as containing indirect untranslatable statements: the narrative of the Fall in Genesis; the first verses of St John's Gospel; the statements of the Last Judgment. We may find parallels among the representatives of 'modernism' or the Sufic tradition in Islam. The great Muslim leader Sir Muhammed Iqbāl (1873–1938) says: 'Heaven and Hell are states, not localities. Their descriptions in the Quran are visual representations of an inner fact, i.e. character. . .'[29] From Indian religion we could probably collect many sentences that could be demonstrated by a simple empirical test to be indirect intranslatable statements: for instance, the following sentences from the *Chandogya Upanisad*; 'In the beginning this (world) was non-existent. It became existent. It grew. It turned into an egg. It lay for the period of a year. It burst open. Then came out of the eggshell two parts, one of silver, the other of gold . . .'[30] *Description 2 difficult* Owing to the uncertainty as to whether ordinary religious men hold any *beliefs* concerning the function of indirect statements, it is difficult to make descriptive hypotheses of category 2. Among the great mystics of all religions, however, we find the theory that what they say about God and the world is true but not literally true, and therefore impossible to express adequately.[31]

An argument designed to show that some sentences, which might belong to the problematic set, can reasonably be used as indirect untranslatable statements We must now consider whether the philosophical argument against the reasonableness of using religious sentences of the problematic set as statements with a localization in the real world could be applied also to the use of the problematic sentences as indirect untranslatable statements.

Braithwaite, as a consequence of his descriptive and con-

[29] Quoted from H. A. R. Gibb, *Modern Trends in Islam*, p.80.

[30] Quoted from Frederick J. Streng, *Emptiness, A Study in Religious Meaning*, Abingdon Press, New York 1967, p.129.

[31] See W. T. Stace, *Mysticism and Philosophy*, Macmillan, London 1961, p.277. Cf. Ninian Smart, who rightly remarks that 'indescribable', 'ineffable', etc., can be a certain sort of intensifier (*Reasons and Faiths*, p.70).

structive theories as outlined above, thinks that the statements of religious language which have a fictitious localization are only indirect expressions. Braithwaite's way of working out this idea is well-known and has often been retold. We now see that his theory as a whole contains true descriptive elements, but that it is mainly a constructive theory which reduces the manifold uses of religious sentences to those compatible with the semantic consequence of the minimum thesis of empiricism. As such it is constructed, in my own view, with a deep sensitivity to the factual use of Christian language.

What Braithwaite does not take into account is the fact that religious men pretend to make indirect untranslatable statements, and are sometimes conscious of their untranslatability. Perhaps he does not think it worthwhile to discuss whether or not there are indirect untranslatable statements. But we shall here outline a theory according to which it is reasonable to make such statements. If this theory is correct, then the minimum thesis of empiricism and similar principles need some qualification and we can recognize in a constructive study of religious language that it is possible in principle to determine whether or not some sentences, which might belong to the problematic set, have an anchorage in the real world. The conclusion of the argument on pp.32f. must in this case be modified.[32]

The theory of importance here stems from the psychology of knowledge. As we shall see, it is very common-sensical, and it has been discussed by Wittgenstein and alluded to by numerous philosophers of religion,[33] who have sometimes drawn far-reaching conclusions from it. This theory may be of importance for the ultimate truth-questions of religion, and we shall return to it later in this book. As regards the question posed in this section, the theory may give an interesting answer but not a dramatic one. To be able to state it adequately, we must start

[32] Cf. on the following I. M. Crombie, 'The Possibility of Theological Statements', in *Faith and Logic*, ed. Basil Mitchell, p.73.
[33] Ludwig Wittgenstein, *Philosophical Investigations*, Basil Blackwell, Oxford 1958 (1959), pp.193ff.

by drawing certain distinctions which will prepare the ground for what is later said about metaphors.[34]

Indirect-metaphorical We must distinguish between an indirect statement, expression, etc., on the one hand, and a metaphorical statement, on the other. A predicate or predicate phrase is said to be a metaphor or to be used metaphorically when it is meaningfully applied to something in such a way that it radically changes its ordinary meaning. This definition lends a certain vagueness to the term 'metaphor' (when is a change of meaning radical?), but this does not matter here. A statement containing a metaphor will be called a metaphorical statement. A classical example of a metaphorical statement is:

(i) Man is a wolf.

This says: it is true for all xs that if x is a man then x has the property of being a wolf in a metaphorical sense. The xs concerned are seen as entities in the real world.

An example of a sentence used as an indirect statement or expression is:

(ii) Every creature that lived before the Fall was naked.

Sometimes such a sentence is also said to have a metaphorical sense. It could be analysed as follows: it is true for all xs that if x is a creature and x lived before the Fall, then x was naked. Here the predicate has no metaphorical sense, but the xs about which something is said do belong to a fictitious world. We shall restrict the term 'metaphorical' to such sentences as (i). Sentence (ii), as used in a Christian context, is in our terminology an indirect sentence.

Now there is a quite well-known theory about the untranslatability of metaphors, namely the interaction theory of I. A. Richards and M. Black.[35] This theory starts from the observation that some metaphorical sentences are impossible to

---

[34] For a general discussion of metaphors providing a good background to what is said in this section and the following see Monroe C. Beardsley, 'The Metaphorical Twist', *Philosophy and Phenomenological Research*, XXII, 1962, pp.293–307.

[35] See Max Black, *Models and Metaphors*, Cornell University Press, New York 1962, pp.38–47.

translate into non-metaphorical sentences without altering their cognitive meaning. The theory then posits a somewhat speculative psychological theory in explanation of this astonishing fact. We shall now take up certain parts of Black's theory, combine it with some connected ideas, and apply it not only to metaphorical but also to indirect sentences. We shall arrive in this way at a theory which seems to be hinted at by some philosophers of religion and which, in the form given here, might show the reasonableness of using indirect untranslatable statements.

Ambiguous object Let us begin by introducing the term 'ambiguous object'. We shall call an object ambiguous when it is possible to experience it in at least two ways, such that to state a description of one way of experiencing the object as the only true description of the object is incompatible with a description of another way of experiencing the object. The psychologically and philosophically well-known duck-rabbit is an ambiguous object. If, seeing it as a duck-picture, we state that it is a duck-picture and not a picture of anything else, then this description is incompatible with saying that it is a picture of a rabbit.

Object with a changing Gestalt Now there are two kinds of ambiguous object of importance here. The first kind we shall call 'objects with a changing *Gestalt*'. The duck-rabbit belongs to this category.

An object with a changing *Gestalt* can be described in different incompatible ways. Sometimes one description is experienced to be true, sometimes another. It is always wrong to state that one of the descriptions is the only true one. A true description of an ambiguous object of the first type is to say that it can be experienced as . . . . . or as . . . . . or as . . . . .

Object with an uncertain Gestalt The second type of ambiguous objects we shall call 'objects with an uncertain *Gestalt*'. These can also be described in different incompatible ways, and we can refer to experience for the truth of all such descriptions.

But, in contrast to the former kind of entity, these entities are such that one and only one of the possible incompatible des-scriptions is the true one. That we do not experience at once that it is true is due to incomplete experience. Either part of the object is not seen, or some structure in the object is not noticed. Taking an example of the same category as the duck-rabbit, we can say that a figure that may be seen either as a picture of a duck or a picture of a rabbit has an uncertain *Gestalt* it if turns out, on closer inspection, to be a picture of a duck. If we are prevented by practical obstacles from making a closer investi-gation of an ambiguous object, it is in practice (but not in principle) impossible to say whether it is an entity with a changing *Gestalt* or with an uncertain *Gestalt*.

I have used here the concept *Gestalt*, but the reader may notice that we are not bound by our usage to accept any of the contro-versial theories of the Gestalt psychologists.

Metaphors and the adjustment of our minds   Our experience of an ambiguous object is sometimes dependent on the special adjustment of our minds. With one kind of adjustment – ideas expectations, etc. – we experience one *Gestalt* and with another adjustment we experience another *Gestalt*. When an entity is described by a metaphor, the ideas and expectations evoked by the metaphorical expression in its ordinary sense might determine our experience of the entity in such a way that we see one *Gestalt* and not another. This sort of description of the function of a metaphor is in line with Black's and Richards' theory. Black says of our sentence (i): 'The wolf-metaphor suppresses some details, emphasizes others – in short, *organizes* our view of man.'[36]

When trying to express the knowledge we have acquired from a metaphorical sentence, we might find it an impossible task without the use of metaphors. The metaphorical sentence is then untranslatable into an unmetaphorical sentence.

Application to indirect sentences   Indirect sentences might have the same function as metaphorical sentences. They state something

[36] Black, op. cit., p.41.

in a fictitious world. When this fictitious world is compared with an ambiguous object in the real world, we might see a *Gestalt* which we have not noticed before. If we call the fictitious world a model, we might say with F. Ferré: 'A model filters the facts.'[37] Trying to express what we have noticed, it is possible that we shall not be able to do so without using an indirect statement. It is then untranslatable. When something is described by a metaphorical or indirect statement, and the metaphor or indirect statement brings us to notice something we have not seen before, we undergo a sudden experience of insight.

A necessary premise and the conclusion We can now take the final step. If the thing described by an untranslatable indirect sentence is an object with an uncertain *Gestalt* and not an object with a changing *Gestalt*, then the indirect untranslatable sentence is a true or false statement which says something about the real world and which it is reasonable to use in our language. The argument does not involve a denial of the minimum thesis of empiricism, but it complicates the process of verification.

Returning to the problematic set of religious sentences, we can say the following. If it is a true descriptive theory that some sentences which seem to belong to the problematic set are indirect untranslatable statements, then our previous arguments have shown that the use of some of the indirect untranslatable statements in religious language is a reasonable use of language. It is important to emphasize 'some of'. The statements must say something about entities of which we have some sense-experience. This is a condition for using the theory of ambiguous objects. In our examples above (p.42), the story of the Fall may contain an indirect statement about the present situation of mankind. It has a function similar to the metaphorical statement: 'Man is a wolf.' The same can be said of the story of the Last Judgment. But what about the prologue

[37] Frederick Ferré, 'Mapping the Logic of Models in Science and Theology', *New Essays on Religious Language*, ed. Dallas M. High, Oxford University Press, New York 1969, p.88.

to the Gospel of St John? It states – perhaps indirectly and
untranslatably – something about the pre-existent Christ. It is
apparent that the theory of ambiguous objects and our way of
expressing experiences of them says nothing about indirect
statements of this kind. They remain meaningless until we find
a real alternative to the minimum thesis of empiricism.[38]

Examples of theories similar to the argument now outlined   A philosopher who has formulated a theory which bears some resemblance to the one just mentioned is Ian Ramsey.[39] In his book
Religious Language he tries to show how certain religious sentences evoke a special kind of situation. His examples of
religious sentences are sometimes similar to indirect untranslatable statements, according to our terminology. One element
in the situation they evoke is sometimes described as seeing a
new *Gestalt*.[40] Ramsey says that suddenly 'the penny drops',
'the ice breaks'.[41]

If we take Ramsey's theory as an attempt to explain how a
certain use of religious language which he has observed could
be a reasonable use of language, it seems correct so far. He
tends, however, to interpret almost all religious sentences
according to his pattern. This might be due to his starting from

---

[38] An analogous argument is to be found in Ronald W. Hepburn's essay
'Poetry and Religious Belief', which is included in Stephen E. Toulmin,
Ronald W. Hepburn, Alasdair MacIntyre, *Metaphysical Beliefs*, SCM Press,
London 1957, p.147.

[39] In *Models and Mystery*, Oxford University Press, London 1964, he
explicitly adopts Black's theory, pp.2ff.

[40] I. T. Ramsey, *Religious Language*, p.24.

[41] Another philosopher who has touched on this function of religious
language in a different context is R. C. Coburn in his article 'A Neglected
Use of Theological Language', *Mind* LXXII, 1963, pp.369–85. He demon-
strates, rightly according to my view, how certain theological sentences
can provide answers to what he calls 'limiting questions' (see pp.371–3) and
says: 'It may be that certain theological sentences carry what might be
called "pictorial" import, i.e., tend to catalyze in those who hear these
sentences uttered a certain perspective or way of looking at things, much as
good metaphors do; and that by virtue of this feature also 'answer' religious
limiting questions by once more removing the disquietude, say, which has
erupted in the asking of such a question' (p.375).

a descriptive theory based on a definition of religious language that is not analytically neutral.[42] In the philosophical parts of his theory he does not sufficiently stress the distinction between statements about empirical and non-empirical ambiguous objects. He thinks that the indirect or metaphorical statements in religious language function in such a way that we not only come to see ourselves or our environment in a new light, but that we also get some sense of the transcendent.[43] This is something that cannot be claimed on the basis of the theory here outlined. In claiming this, Ramsey in fact hints at another theory to which we shall return.

Many theories of religious knowledge start from the observation of the ambiguous character of certain entities. An obvious example is John Hick's essay 'Religious Faith as Experiencing-as'.[44] We shall return to these theories when considering alternatives to the minimum thesis of empiricism in Chapter V. As regards the narrower problem of the function of indirect religious sentences, they have little to say.

Application to the phenomenon of changing localization Having now discussed a possible way of explaining and justifying the use of some sentences of the problematic set as indirect statements in religious language, we can attempt an explanation of the phenomenon of the changing localization of religious sentences. Let us observe that a sentence which is a true statement with its localization in the real world can be applied to a wider area

[42] It is possible that he stipulates which situations are religious in a way which fits his analysis.

[43] *Religious Language*, for example p. 129. Many writers on religious metaphors have noticed that the metaphors have, according to the believers, some relation to a transcendent reality. R. F. Aldwinckle, for example, says: 'The religious consciousness, however, always considers the symbol to contain a non-symbolic element, i.e., it refers to a transcendent reality which exists. Hence "the religious symbol is, then, in its essence – and epistemologically – metaphysical in character, although psychologically it is more akin to poetry".' 'Myth and Symbol in Contemporary Philosophy and Theology', *The Journal of Religion* XXXV, 1954, p.268. Aldwinckle's quotation is from W. M. Urban, *Language and Reality*, Macmillan, New York 1951, p.581.

[44] *Talk of God*, pp.20–35.

of reality. This is the case when the sentence primarily describes an event which has happened in the real world, and the description of this event determines, for instance, our experience of human life in such a way that we come to grasp a new pattern in it. The second truth expressed by the statement can stand, even if we should find that the description of the actual event to be false. A novel by Zola may contain historically true statements, but these statements also have something to say about human life in general, regardless of their historical truth or falsehood. This means that a sentence can be a statement with two kinds of independent truth-claims in respect of the real world. We shall call such sentences 'statements with a twofold truth-claim'. First, the sentence claims to be true as an ordinary direct statement with its localization in the real world. Secondly, it tries to reveal a more general truth in respect of the real world. The second truth-claim is the same as the truth-claim which an indirect statement can contain in respect of the real world. It can be explained in the same way as that in which we have just attempted to explain indirect statements. If the first truth-claim is not fulfilled, then the sentence can be said to have a fictitious localization and to be an indirect statement.

Many religious sentences seem to be statements with a twofold truth-claim. The Creation story and the narrative of the birth of Jesus may have this character, in many religious groups. We can now guess that this was the case for the men who first used the narratives, and that they were not conscious of the problems relating to the first truth-claim. When, however, these began to emerge, it was evident to religious men that the important truth of the narratives was the second one. They could therefore to some extent neglect the first truth-claim.[45] It is the same thing not to be interested in the first truth-claim of the narratives as to lack interest in their localization. If this speculative hypothesis concerning the development of certain

[45] This agrees *mutatis mutandis* with the theory of the development of mythological thinking which Macquarrie formulates in discussing Bultmann. See John Macquarrie, *God-Talk, An Examination of the Language and Logic of Theology*, SCM Press, London 1967, pp.173ff.

central Christian narratives is correct, then this could explain the astonishing lack of interest we have noticed among some Christians in the localization of religious statements. It remains, however, a fact that deep, concealed disagreements exist between men in the same religious tradition as to the localization of certain statements. One man finds religious importance in a sentence which is a direct statement about the real world, while another finds the same sentence important only as an indirect statement.

How can we know if the reasoning in this section is correct? How can we know if the reasoning outlined from p.42 onwards is correct? We meet here what was called above an explanatory theory, and we are consequently in the field of empirical science. The argument is intended to indicate the causes of a certain semantic fact – namely the untranslatability and communicative power of certain metaphors and indirect sentences. In doing so, it embraces certain other explanatory theories in the psychology of knowledge and perception. It is possible to make the theory as a whole more precise, to test its consequences experimentally, and to judge its explanatory merits. This is done only for certain specific traits but, on the face of it, the theory seems to have a certain plausibility. The distinctions we have made in presenting it will be of importance in our closing chapter. Our argument, however, was not designed purely to explain certain mechanisms underlying our linguistic behaviour. It was primarily an attempt to justify the knowledge-claim of the speech-acts concerned. This end will have been achieved if the explanation connected the use of metaphorical and indirect statements with processes which we already recognize as a legitimate way of acquiring and expressing knowledge, or which we are willing so to recognize upon reflection. Even this second test may prove favourable to the theory, and it therefore exemplifies a reasonable belief concerning religious language.

6. Does any theory of metaphors or symbols or analogies or models solve the problem of religious statements?

Restriction to the problem of a cognitive function of untranslatable metaphors It is not our purpose here to analyse the vast discussion of metaphors, symbols, analogies, etc., in religious language. We have briefly considered a theory of metaphors in the previous section. We shall now ask whether there are any other theories which can provide a solution to the problems of religious statements observed above. This means that we can make, from the beginning, two important restrictions: we shall discuss only the cognitive function of metaphors, etc., and only such sentences – if there are any – which it is impossible to translate into a language without metaphors, etc.

Terminology The terminology in this field changes within different philosophical schools and different periods. We have already defined metaphor, metaphorical sentence and indirect sentence. In our terminology, we need none of the other terms in the heading. Analogy, for instance, can be described as a special form of metaphor.

Descriptive observations We have discussed above whether we could say descriptively that religious language contains untranslatable indirect statements, and we said that it probably does. With the method outlined in the discussion of indirect statements, we could probably also establish whether or not the factual use of nearly all religious languages involves untranslatable metaphorical statements.

An empirical study could also confirm certain other hypotheses relating to the use of metaphorical and indirect sentences in different religious languages. Let us take an example from Christian language. As is apparent from the description on p.44, a metaphor is applied to a certain subject mentioned in a metaphorical statement. An indirect statement, on the contrary, can be applied to different areas of reality. Its field of application is not given by the statement itself. Indirect statements in Christian language are regularly applied to different areas of reality. The story of the Virgin Birth is often used as an indirect statement of something unique about the birth of Jesus. But the story is also applied to the believer himself. It is then supposed to state indirectly something about the origin of faith in Christian men.[46] This changing application of indirect statements, or of statements having a twofold truth-claim, is systemized in the classical fourfold interpretation of the Bible.[47]

Three theories which explain the use of metaphors only if we accept the possibility of knowledge of something transcendent. (i) An inter-action theory The theory outlined in connection with Black was a serious attempt to explain and justify the use of untranslatable indirect and metaphorical sentences. However, many religious men meeting this theory would surely reject it. They would say that religion gives us knowledge of quite another kind of reality, and that this cannot be explained on the basis of a theory like that mentioned above. The theories discussed here all attempt to explain how we talk metaphorically or indirectly about a reality quite different from the world of everyday experiences.

The first theory is a development of certain thoughts in Black's theory. It is to be found, for example, in Ramsey (cf. above p.49). According to this theory, the metaphorical or indirect statement not only helps us to see new aspects of empirical reality, but also organizes our knowledge of this world by the mechanism described above, so that we become aware of its relation to a trans-empirical reality. In order to take this theory seriously, we must reckon with the possibility of trans-empirical knowledge. If this is reasonable, the theory

[46] For a background to this type of thinking in Roman Catholic theology and liturgy see Thomas Aquinas, *S. Theol.*, III, 28, 1, C.

[47] A standard example of this method of scriptural exegesis is the interpretation of sentences containing the word 'Jerusalem'. They can be interpreted not only to say something about a certain earthly place but also about the Christian church (*sensus allegoricus*), about the soul of man (*sensus tropologicus*) and about the heavenly city (*sensus anagogicus*). See further Beryl Smalley, *The Study of the Bible in the Middle Ages*, Basil Blackwell, Oxford 1952. Smalley comments on the example concerning 'Jerusalem' on p.28.

might explain the fact that religious men make untranslatable metaphorical or indirect statements, the explanation being one that a religious believer could accept. In our last chapter we shall analyse theories of religious or trans-empirical knowledge from the starting point of the argument stated on p.32. Following that discussion, we shall return to this theory of metaphors.

(ii) The theory of circumstantial metaphors   A quite different theory, and one not generally discussed in connection with religious language, also becomes of great interest if one accepts the supposition that there are cognitive religious experiences. We sometimes describe an experience by describing the situation in which we have it. Let us take a simple example: 'Happiness is a warm puppy.' What is said by this sentence can be interpreted as follows: Imagine that you were in the situation of having a warm puppy in your arms. The peculiar experience which you have in such a situation is what I mean by 'happiness'. The expression 'a warm puppy' in our example is a metaphor. Let us call it a 'circumstantial metaphor'. If the experience described by a circumstantial metaphor cannot be described in any other way, then a sentence containing a circumstantial metaphor is an example of an untranslatable metaphorical sentence, the function of which we know. If, now, there is a cognitive religious experience, we can guess that some untranslatable metaphorical religious sentences are statements containing a circumstantial metaphor. The metaphor in this case indicates a situation in which the religious experience can be achieved. The sentence 'God is in his holy temple' occurs at the beginning of many Christian services. In its ordinary meaning – i.e. in ascribing to God a specific spatial place – it is, of course, false for all Christians. It can, however, be interpreted as containing a circumstantial metaphor. It is then a shorter way of saying: 'The experience you may have in the quietness of a church is the indescribable experience of the presence of God.'

A variant: situation-creating sentences   We shall now observe that the sentence quoted above can not only be used to point out a situation. It is normally used to create a situation of worship.

A defining characteristic of a religious sentence is, according to what we have said in Chapter I, that it should be part of what constitutes a religious situation. Imagine now that a religious situation is created by the utterance of certain sentences, as for instance in a hymn, which do not contain a single direct or indirect or metaphorical statement which religious men engaged in the situation would hold to be true. The believers can still say that they are communicating some inexpressible knowledge of the transcendent by participation in the situation. Whether or not this case exists is a matter of empirical research. I think it does.[48] The believer's position is not unreasonable if there are cognitive religious experiences. Just as it seems possible to express a cognitive experience by a circumstantial metaphor, so too may it be possible to express the experience by creating a certain situation. When the meaning of a religious sentence stems only from its function of creating a religious situation, we shall call it a 'situation-creating sentence'. Given the possibility of an experience of the transcendent, these sentences might be statements of a kind which is neither indirect nor metaphorical according to our terminology, but which resembles both.

(iii) The theory of analogy The best-known explanation of the function of untranslatable metaphorical statements about God is the Thomistic theory of analogy. A summary of this can be found in every textbook in the philosophy of religion. For the theory to work, we must know that there is some kind of likeness between something in the world (for instance wisdom) and God. In St Thomas, this supposition caused no problems because he accepted the Neo-Platonic scale of being as a well-grounded truth about the world. We can follow how, in the eighteenth century, the theory of analogy became problematic when the Neo-Platonic metaphysics was disputed. The interesting thing for us in this chapter is that the theory of analogy, as an explanation of the cognitive functions of some

---

[48] Cf. what Ninian Smart calls the engineering function of certain religious formulas, *Reasons and Faiths*, p.102.

untranslatable metaphorical statements about God, does not work without a premise stating some kind of likeness between God and the world.[49] This premise is then a candidate for the problematic set of sentences. This theory of analogy, therefore, cannot itself solve any of the fundamental problems of religious sentences, although it may prove valuable if these problems could be solved by any other theory. The same criticism can possibly be made in regard to most of the famous theories of symbols in religious language. We shall shortly discuss Tillich as an example.

Discussion of Tillich's theory of symbols   I am not sure whether there is only *one* theory of symbols in Tillich. Possibly he has several interwoven theories. We shall formulate here one line of thought which seems to be present in Tillich's main works.

Tillich's description of symbols shows that a symbolic sentence by his conception must be characterized, in our terminology, as an indirect statement or sometimes as a metaphorical one. These symbolic sentences can be understood as ordinary statements in our everyday language. We see what it means, for instance, to ascribe wisdom to a being and, consequently, we easily understand the sentence 'God is wise'. But this statement in its ordinary meaning has, according to Tillich, no anchorage in the real world. There is no such being as is talked about in the statement.[50] Its anchorage is fictitious and the

---

[49] See Anders Jeffner, *Butler and Hume on Religion. A Comparative Analysis*, Acta Universitatis Upsaliensis, Diakonistyrelsens bokförlag, Stockholm 1966, pp.175–88. Cf. Stace, *Mysticism and Philosophy*, p.293. Perhaps we could say that the premise concerning the likeness between God and the world works in such a way that it connects the language about God with the language about the world. Thereby these two areas of the language come to belong to what Waismann calls the same 'language-stratum'. A discussion relevant to this question is William P. Alston's critique of the 'whittle-down method' in 'The Elucidation of Religious Statements', *Process and Divinity, The Hartshorne Festschrift*, ed. William L. Reese, Open Court, LaSalle, Ill. 1964, pp.429–43.

[50] Concerning Tillich's view that we often think about God in a concrete way and that there is no such being as we think about in this way see his *Dynamics of Faith*, George Allen and Unwin, London 1957, pp.46f.

statement is false, if seen as localized in the real world. If, however, we realize that the statement is symbolic, then we can find that it is true. In our terminology, it is an indirect statement.[51] Tillich obviously sees many symbolic sentences as statements. He himself often uses the term 'assertion', and explicitly states that symbolic sentences give knowledge. An important point is that religious symbolic sentences are untranslatable. According to Tillich, you cannot say in a non-symbolic sentence what is said in a symbolic one.[52]

What is now of interest is how Tillich describes the mechanism which allows a sentence with a fictitious localization or an ordinary empirical statement to say something true about an indescribable reality. Tillich seems to mean that this is due partly to the fact that the symbol participates in what is symbolized.[53] To understand this we must know what is meant by 'symbol' and 'participation', and this is not at all clear in Tillich's text.

A symbol seems to be certain existing properties or entities or ideas in the real world.[54] In saying that 'Father' is a symbol, Tillich must mean that the property of being a father is a symbol. It is not the terms which are symbols, strictly speaking, but what the terms stand for. All terms – with the probable exception of onomatopoeic terms – must, according to Tillich's terminology, be signs.

Tillich's use of the term 'participation' is very embarrassing. In his *Systematic Theology* he says that every relation includes a kind of participation.[55] But he states elsewhere that a sign does not participate in the reality of that to which it points.[56] We are not going to discuss the several meanings of participation in Tillich's texts, but we will try to define a relation which he

---

[51] Some symbolic sentences are statements having a twofold truth-claim (see above p.50). Whether or not the first truth-claim of a symbolic sentence is fulfilled is irrelevant, Tillich says. *Systematic Theology*, Vol. I, Nisbet, Welwyn 1951, p.266.

[52] See, for instance, *Dynamics of Faith*, p.44.

[53] *Dynamics of Faith*, p.42.

[54] Ibid. Cf. *Systematic Theology* I, p.132.

[55] Op. cit., p.196.　　　　[56] *Dynamics of Faith*, p.42.

might have had in mind when saying that the symbol participates in what it symbolizes.

In trying to interpret the particular form of participation
which exists between a symbol and what is symbolized, it may
be helpful to observe how Tillich compares and distinguishes
symbols from signs and symptoms. The differences between a
sign and a symbol are explained by Tillich in many places. One
such difference – mentioned above – is that a sign does not
participate in the reality of which it is a sign. It is important for
Tillich to spell out the differences, because signs and symbols
also have an important characteristic in common – they point
beyond themselves to something else. We shall not here consider
further the discussion of signs, but instead observe the relations
between symbols and symptoms.[57] This latter distinction is
not so common in Tillich, and not so much discussed by the
commentators. An example, according to Tillich, of a symptom which ought not to be confused with a symbol is the
so-called dream-symbol (*Traumsymbol*).[58] One important difference seems to be that what is indicated by a symptom may be
something trivial, which can be known and described without
having access to the symptom, but the real symbol will always
allow us to discover new dimensions of reality that cannot be
grasped directly. This means that the symbol-relation involves
more than the mere symptom-relation, but it does not say that
these two relations have nothing in common. Tillich surely
thinks that they have, just as do signs and symbols. It is now no
great step to interpret Tillich as suggesting that precisely the
relation of participation which holds between the symbol and
what it symbolizes is a special form of symptom-relation. Let us
offer an example of a symptom-relation which is of importance
for our purposes. A rash of a certain kind is a symptom of

[57] See for an example of this distinction P. Tillich, 'The Meaning and
Justification of Religious Symbols', in *Religious Experience and Truth*, ed.
Sidney Hook, Oliver and Boyd, Edinburgh 1962, p.3.
[58] This example is added by Tillich in the German edition of the essay
'The Meaning and Justification of Religious Symbols'. See P. Tillich,
Die Frage nach dem Unbedingten (Gesammelte Werke, Band V. Herausgegeben
von Renate Albrecht), Evangelisches Verlagswerk, Stuttgart 1964, p.237.

scarlet fever. It is not the same to have a rash as to have scarlet fever, but if we have scarlet fever this explains why we have a rash. The rash is also a property of this disease, although it is possible sometimes to have scarlet fever without a rash. If S is a symptom of A in this sense of 'symptom', then S is not identical with A; the occurrence of A is a necessary condition for the occurrence of S and S is a property of A, although not a constitutive one. When, in the following pages, we speak of 'symptoms', we shall do so in the special sense now explained. A symptom in this sense can in trivial cases stand for the process or entity of which it is a symptom. If two of the children have had scarlet fever with a rash, and I say to my wife, 'Now the third child has a rash', this sentence means the same as 'Now the third child has scarlet fever'. In this case 'rash' has many properties in common with a symbol in Tillich's sense, but it is not a symbol because of the fairly trivial knowledge we obtain from it. (There are also other requirements of a symbol which it does not fulfil.) Our suggestion now is that the relation of participation which is one of the relations constituting a symbol should be interpreted in certain important contexts as the relation of being a symptom in the sense here explained.

We can now return to the indirect statements of religion. The level of reality about which they can say something indirectly cannot be talked of directly: it can be neither described nor indicated, but we can have some sort of experience of it. Tillich calls this Being itself or the Absolute or God.[59]

Now it sometimes happens that we recognize that our ideas, or something in our real world, participate in Being itself. Or, in our translation, that something appears to be a symptom of the indescribable reality.[60] When we then talk about this

[59] The sentence 'God is Being itself' is not symbolic according to Tillich. This does not contradict his view that we cannot say something directly about the Ultimate Reality. The sentence simply equates two names for this unspeakable level of existence. If we have some concrete idea of God as an existing being with some properties, this idea is a symbol for Being itself, or, which is the same, for God: 'God is a symbol for God' (*Dynamics of Faith*, p.46).

[60] This is possible, Tillich thinks, because everything that exists or is

symptom which we have recognized, we speak symbolically about Being itself. When, for instance, we say about God that he is almighty, we talk directly about a highest Being who can do as he pleases.[61] There is, however, no such Being. Our idea, however, can be recognized as a symptom of Being itself or God and, therefore, the fictitious statement 'God is almighty' asserts something about a level of reality in a way analogous to that in which a statement about a rash can indirectly assert something about scarlet fever.

Tillich thinks it is impossible to know in advance what things or ideas can be recognized as symptoms of the indescribable level of reality. We cannot, therefore, construct symbols or determine which religious sentences are symbolic and true.

Tillich's theory – an explanatory theory based on the supposition that a sentence of the problematic set is a statement with its location in the real world   If someone wishes to accept Tillich's theory, then he must accept a sentence of the following kind: 'There is a certain relation – being a symptom of – between something in this world or an imagined world and an indescribable reality of a kind quite different from that which we experience in our daily life.' This is a sentence of the problematic set which cannot be explained by the theory, and we are back to the problem of these sentences as it emerges in the argument on p.32.

Even if we adopt a different interpretation of Tillich's theory of symbols from that given here, it is obvious that the theory is based on a sentence of the problematic set.

An interpretation of Bultmann's theory of myths   We have noticed above a constructive theory which, for theological reasons, referred all or nearly all religious sentences in the Christian tradition to the problematic set. As an example, we gave an account of some arguments from Bultmann. We have also seen

---

imagined participates in Being itself. How Tillich knows this, he does not tell us, but his theory of symbol works without this far-reaching assumption.

[61] *Dynamics of Faith*, p.47.

that the myths in Bultmann's theory are statements with a fictitious localization, but statements which say something about reality. It is now no great step to interpret Bultmann as saying that the myths are indirect untranslatable statements of the type discussed above (pp.42–47), i.e. that they reveal a pattern in reality which it is impossible to indicate and talk about without indirect statements. The following quotation from Bultmann fits such an interpretation. Bultmann says of the revelation:

'What, then, has been revealed? Nothing at all, so far as the question concerning revelation asks for doctrines – doctrines, say, that no man could have discovered for himself – or for mysteries that become known once and for all as soon as they are communicated. On the other hand, however, *everything has been revealed, insofar as man's eyes are opened concerning his own existence and he is once again able to understand himself*. It is as Luther says: "Thus, in going out of himself, God brings it about that we go into ourselves; and through knowledge of him he brings us to knowledge of ourselves".'[62]

With this interpretation, the same difficulties emerge in Bultmann's theology as we have noted in our discussion of Ramsey. If the indirect statements of religion reveal a certain *Gestalt* in the empirical world of man, this is something quite different from saying something about God. Bultmann, however, thinks that we acquire some kind of knowledge of God through indirect statements. He even says that God-sentences are analogous.[63] These kinds of difficulty in Bultmann's theory are clearly indicated by Macquarrie.[64] Possibly Bultmann means that the myths, when applied to reality, cause an experience of the transcendent in the way we described when adding to Black's theory a supposition of trans-empirical knowledge (p.53).

[62] Rudolf Bultmann, *Existence and Faith*, Hodder & Stoughton, London 1961, pp.85f.

[63] Rudolf Bultmann, *Jesus Christ and Mythology*, p.68. The same point is made in *Kerygma und Mythos*, II Band, Herausgegeben von H. W. Bartsch, Herbert Reich, Evangelischer Verlag, Hamburg 1952, p.196.

[64] John Macquarrie, *God-Talk*, pp.40f.

Another interpretation which gives a new kind of theory – trans-empirical symptoms The above line of interpretation of Bult-mann may be partially correct. Sometimes, however, Bult-mann seems to hint at a quite different theory, according to which some sentences in religious language belong to a category of sentences impossible to describe with the common semantical terminology. We shall try to give an outline of such a theory. If some religious sentences are neither statements, nor expressions, nor prescriptions, nor performatives, what are they? To clarify this point, let us look at a theory in the early Wittgenstein.

Ethical, aesthetical and religious sentences are nonsense, according to the early Wittgenstein's well-known theory of language. They do not state anything about reality either directly or indirectly. Wittgenstein, however, thinks that there is something outside the limits of our language, namely some *a priori* order of the world.[65] Wittgenstein, now, is not absolutely silent about this ineffable order. He seems to ascribe some communicative power to the nonsensical sentences of ethics, aesthetics and religion. He uses these sentences himself, and he seems to think that they are interchangeable.[66] But how could nonsensical sentences express any kind of cognition? Wittgen-stein never tells us what he thinks about this. We have to guess. Could it not be that the use of this nonsense may be recognized as a symptom of the unspeakable level of reality in the same way as things and concepts are recognized as symptoms according to our interpretation of Tillich? Let us follow this line of thought. In Tillich, symbolic sentences were statements about something that could reveal the unspeakable reality. According to the theory suggested here, the very usage of certain sentences which are not statements at all, is a symptom of the unspeak-able. We can describe Tillich without introducing any new

[65] Wittgenstein's early theory of religion is clearly analysed in a Danish book: Jens Glebe Möller, *Wittgenstein og Religionen* (Wittgenstein and Religion), Gads Forlag, Köbenhavn 1969. See here the summary on pp.91ff. and especially pp.40f., where Möller quotes from Wittgenstein's *Tagebücher* 1:6. 1915 and comments on *Tractatus* 5.634.

[66] Möller, op. cit., for example p.90, where he refers – among many other texts – to *Tractatus* 6.421.

kind of linguistic entity. But here we have to mark out a special category for nonsensical sentences which have the property of being recognizable as symptoms of the unspeakable. Let us call these kinds of speech-acts 'trans-empirical symptoms'. We can think of such a linguistic category also on the basis of other theories of language than that presented in the *Tractatus*.

It seems now to be correct to say that one line of thought in Bultmann is to see Christian religious language as consisting partly of trans-empirical symptoms. The reality that it indicates cannot be talked about in statements, since it cannot be made an object. Still, the religious language is itself a symptom of a reality outside the world of facts. There is, Bultmann seems to say, another class of sentences which can also be used as trans-empirical symptoms. They can be found in the language which has its origin in our own 'existence', and which is used and analysed by the existentialist philosophers.[67] To speak of my authentic existence is not to make statements – not even symbolic or metaphorical statements. According to the existentialist tradition this talk is more like a symptom of an unspeakable level of human reality.[68] Bultmann seems to mean

[67] R. Bultmann, *Jesus Christ and Mythology*, pp.56ff. Cf. *Kerygma und Mythos*, II Band, where Bultmann says, p.187: 'Es . . gibt eine Sprache, in der sich Existenz naiv ausspricht, und es gibt entsprechend eine Wissenschaft, die ohne die Existenz zum welthaften Sein zu objektivieren, von der Existenz redet.' Stuart C. Brown, in his book *Do Religious Claims Make Sense?*, SCM Press, London 1969, interprets Bultmann as holding the view that religious sentences are possible to understand without being a believer. According to our interpretation here, one must have some experience of the transcendent to be able to recognize a trans-empirical symptom. This does not contradict Brown's interpretation, because Bultmann thinks that we have in the experience of our own existence such special experience of a reality outside the world of scientific statements which makes it possible to understand what a trans-empirical symptom might be a symptom of. Cf. Bultmann's 'Das Problem der Hermeneutik', *Zeitschrift für Theologie und Kirche* XLVII, 1950, pp.66f.

[68] One of the existentialist philosophers who has deeply influenced Bultmann is Martin Heidegger. Heidegger, in his very complicated theory of language, seems to ascribe, particularly to poetic language, those characteristics which have led us to talk about transcendental symptoms. Some sentences from the great poets, which reveal the deepest levels of being can neither be characterized as metaphorical statements or as expressions, if we follow Heidegger. In *Erläuterungen zu Hölderins Dichtung*, Vittorio

that Christian religious language is a symptom of a new dimension of this unspeakable reality. But, if this interpretation is correct, how could Bultmann say – as he does in fact say – that God-sentences are analogical?[69] To say something about God analogically in the usual meaning of that term is to make a statement about God. But Bultmann perhaps does not mean more by his talk of analogy than that the symptoms are symptoms of a realm of *reality*. He is concerned to defend his view from the theory that sentences about God are nothing but statements with a fictitious localization. Erich Frank, to whom Bultmann refers, says that the difference between an analogy and a metaphor consists in the fact that an analogy reflects the true reality.[70]

Let us summarize this line of interpretation of Bultmann. A Christian sentence such as 'God sent his Son into the world' will be analysed thus. It is a statement with a fictitious localization constituting a myth. Sometimes it is seen as a statement with its localization in the real world. As such it is obviously false. Used as a religious sentence it is still important, and a religious man can use it meaningfully. It then belongs to the problematic set. However, it is neither an indirect statement nor an indirect expression. It is a trans-empirical symptom.

Comparison with Zurdeeg There is another theory which is in many ways very different from Bultmann's, but which seems to contain a line of thought similar to that just referred to. This is the theory put forward by W. F. Zurdeeg in his book *An Analytical Philosophy of Religion*. Zurdeeg explicitly denies that

---

Klostermann, Frankfurt am Main 1951, he says: 'Das Gedicht "drückt" nicht "Erlebnisse" des Dichters "aus"', sondern nimmt den Dichter hinein in den als Gedicht eröffneten Bezirk seines Wesens' (p.142). See further Irmgard Bock, *Heideggers Sprachdenken*, Verlag Anton Hein, Meisenheim am Glan 1966. Bock, however, points out that 'Dichtung' means more than poetry or fiction in Heidegger's works. 'Sie [Dichtung] kann in der Poesie, aber genau so gut in der Gesetzgebung, in Mythos oder Kultus geschehen' (p.56).

[69] See above, note 63.

[70] Erich Frank, *Philosophical Understanding and Religious Truth*, Oxford University Press, London 1946, pp.163f.

religious language contains any ordinary empirical statements.[71] All sentences having the form of statements belong to the problematic set. The function of these sentences is neither that of indirect metaphorical statements nor of expressions. Zurdeeg tries to define a special category to which he refers religious sentences. This category he calls 'convictional language'.[72] Convictional language is a behaviour grounded in a special experience of being overcome. This is not the same as being convinced of the truth of some hypothesis about the world. And it is not just adopting a certain perspective on the world or expressing a certain state of mind, even if it is to a great extent the latter activity.[73] Zurdeeg sometimes argues as if convictional language were absolutely non-cognitive,[74] but his main line of argument seems to be that the ordinary categories 'cognitive – non-cognitive' are impossible to apply to convictional language.[75] We cannot *argue* for or against what is said in a certain conventional language. But by a certain base-experience we can begin to talk it. This talk is then a behaviour caused by the experience, a symptom of a human state of being.[76] It is possible to think about these linguistic symptoms and then attempt to order them according to certain rules (though not, of course, logical ones). This is the task of theologians and of those developing any ideology.[77] Zurdeeg does not define the base-experience, but he seems to regard it as some kind of experience of reality as whole.[78]

Even these theories presuppose the truth of one of the problematic sentences What is problematic, from our point of view, in this kind of theory is obvious. It is the same difficulty as was noted above in the commentary on Tillich. One tries to give an

[71] He says 'indicative language'. See Willem F. Zurdeeg, *An Analytical Philosophy of Religion*, George Allen and Unwin, London 1959, pp.44 ff.

[72] Zurdeeg, op. cit., p.19.

[73] Zurdeeg, op. cit., p.61.

[74] Zurdeeg, op. cit., pp.23ff.

[75] Zurdeeg, op. cit. pp.54f. Note the term 'understanding'.

[76] Zurdeeg speaks about 'linguistic aspects of our living', op. cit., p.56.

[77] Zurdeeg, op. cit., p.304.

[78] Zurdeeg, op. cit., p.45 (cf. p.132).

explanation of how a set of problematic sentences can be used meaningfully. In working out this explanation, one has to use one of the problematic sentences, e.g. 'There is something transcendent.'[79] Zurdeeg does not make any decision as to which convictional language is the right one. If, however, we want to accept Zurdeeg's theory and use it as an explanation of how some religious sentences can be cognitive and, at the same time, belong to the problematic set, we have to accept a sentence which is in itself of the problematic kind as, for example, the following: 'A man speaking a religious convictive language may have been overcome by an experience of a reality outside the realm of empirical science.' It does not follow from what has now been said that these theories are wrong, but it does follow that they cannot alone explain how we may reasonably use certain sentences as religious men believe themselves to do.

What kind of research can determine whether or not any of the symbol theories are correct?   Let us suppose that we could find some other reason than those given in the symbol-theories for accepting a statement of the problematic set. We may still find it necessary to explain the use of other sentences of the problematic set according to some of the theories outlined in this section. Which criteria shall we use in this situation to be able to find out whether or not any one of them is correct? This will depend on how the theories are used. If they are intended as explanations of the factual use of language among religious men, then we are in the field of empirical science. We have to judge their explanatory power, and this is a difficult task. Often, however, these theories seem to be used almost as constructive ones. The aim is to suggest an interpretation of factual language which will make it more rational, without being in opposition to

[79] Wittgenstein was aware of this. Therefore, he tries to avoid both using religious sentences and theories about this kind of nonsense, but he does not completely succeed. The result is that, in A. Wedberg's words, he opens the window to the transcendent and shuts it at the same time (Anders Wedberg, *Filosofins historia, Från Bolzano till Wittgenstein*, Bonniers, Stockholm 1966, p.188).

fundamental traits of its factual use. If we see the symbol-theories in this way, they are designed to explain, by referring to well-known or understandable processes, how certain sentences of the problematic set should be interpreted in order for them not to be in conflict with science and common sense and in accordance with certain theological standards. If we agree as to the theological standards, then we can judge their relative success by logic and scientific knowledge. But the fundamental problem remains. We need a justification of the basic sentences which belong to the problematic set, and are still statements to which these theories do not apply.

III

RELIGIOUS EXPRESSIONS AND PRESCRIPTIONS

Introduction The numerous discussions of religious language relate, for the most part, to the problem of religious statements. There are few analyses of non-cognitive religious sentences. What are generally called non-cognitive theories of religious language are those which claim that all or most religious sentences are non-cognitive, but they very seldom contain attempts to analyse in more detail the problem of non-cognitive religious sentences. It is thought, possibly, that such sentences are unproblematical. This, however, is not the case. As we shall see, the use of non-cognitive religious sentences poses many problems for discussion. We shall formulate some of these problems and a number of hypothetical solutions. The main interest in this chapter, as in the former, is to indicate what method can be used to obtain an answer to the various questions involved. This task will determine the disposition of the chapter.

On p.11 we introduced a terminology by which a sentence expressing emotive or conative states of mind was called an expression. We shall begin by discussing religious expressions.

Among religious expressions, we find expressions of emotive and conative impulses in the religious believer: . . . 'We praise thee, O God. . .' There is, however, also a category of expressions, the subject of which is God or some supernatural being: The seraphim said: 'Holy, holy, holy is the Lord of hosts.' There are two sets of sentences that may belong to the first category, but which will be discussed separately because they raise special philosophical problems. Those are expressions of moral values and what will be called expressions of perspective. We can divide our discussion of religious expressions into the following sections:

1. Expressions of emotive and conative impulses in religious men;
2. Expressions of emotive and conative impulses in God or supernatural beings;
3. Sentences expressing a perspective;
4. Examples of problems raised by an emotive theory of value.

What we are going to say about expressions can in many cases be applied to prescriptions. It seems superfluous to work out this application. When discussing religious prescriptions in the last paragraph, we will therefore consider only certain new questions which emerge when we try to analyse prescriptions.

1. Expressions of emotive and conative impulses in religious men

A. Questions to be answered empirically (i–iii)   The study of religious expressions is largely a task for empirical psychology. Let us here distinguish between two main fields (i and ii) of psychological research. In the first field we shall note three questions to be answered (*a–c*), and in the second field two such questions (*a–b*). There are other empirical questions besides those of a psychological nature, and these will be discussed at the end of this section (iii).

(i) Description and explanation of the emotional processes   (i) A psychological inquiry can be directed towards the different emotional states of mind which are reflected by the use of a religious language. The task of the psychologist is (*a*) to describe these often very complicated processes, and (*b*) to give an explanation of their genesis. There are well-known theories in this field, from Freud onwards.[1] Although this is a study whose

---

[1] For a survey of these theories see for instance Hjalmar Sundén, *Die Religion und die Rollen. Eine psychologische Untersuchung der Frömmigkeit*, Alfred Töpelmann, Berlin 1966. This book also contains an original contribution to the psychology of religion. We shall come back to it later on, since it has relevance for some of the epistemological questions.

material is partly religious language, we must ignore it in our present context. To enter such a discussion would involve a prolonged discussion of different approaches to the psychology of religion.

Analysis of religious psychology – a neglected task   There is, however, a third question worth noticing, and one which is often forgotten. In analogy to our previous division of descriptive problems, we may ask (*c*): What emotions do religious men think they are expressing when they are using their religious language? To answer this question we must collect some common religious expressions and ask the believers what feelings they are expressing when they use them. By such an inquiry we shall obtain a collection of terms and concepts. If we remove those concepts which belong either to scientific or to everyday psychology, then we shall obtain a psychology of religious men, or 'religious psychology'. Probably all great religions contain fragments of a conceptual apparatus that makes it possible to speak of the emotional states of mind reflected by the religious language. It is, I think, of scientific interest to analyse religious psychological concepts. How can they be analysed by the concepts of an empirical psychology? Do they reveal functions of the mind not observed by empirical psychology or impossible to describe in its terminology? Are such concepts theoretical constructions of importance for our description of human reactions?

If we wish to formulate some hypothetical answer to any of these questions, then I think we could safely say yes to the last of them. There seem to be highly complex emotional states or processes, or combinations of emotional and cognitive attitudes about which it is difficult to talk without using such biblical concepts as faith, or conversion (*metanoia*). The same seems to be true of the state of spiritual consciousness called *tyrīa* in the *Māndūkya Upanisad*.

(ii) The association between the emotional processes and linguistic units
(ii) A psychological study of religious expressions can relate not only to the emotional or conative impulses as such, but to

the association between the actual linguistic sentences and different mental processes. The question then is what sentences express which of the different emotional or conative states of mind studied according to (i) *a* and *b* in certain religious men or groups of religious men. Scientific techniques for such a study exist. I am thinking here mainly of the semantical differential method of Charles Osgood.[2] Osgood and his team start from an interpretation of meaning according to a stimulus-response scheme.[3] They then work out a test which makes it possible to characterize with a certain value on different scales the process they call meaning – expressed and evoked by a given word in a given person or group of persons. Osgood's study is concerned with single *words*, more or less regardless of the situation in which they are used. We are discussing *sentences* of a kind defined by reference to a certain situation. However, it seems that a method similar to Osgood's could be applied to religious sentences read in church, such as: 'Great is the Lord, and highly to be praised' (Ps. 48).

What could be measured in this way are the mental processes or states which we have called emotional or conative. It seems of little importance whether we call this 'meaning' or 'properties of the meaning' or something else. It is also possible to interpret these processes by other models than the S–R machinery, without changing the actual technique of measurement.

Some tasks for a study using a technique similar to Osgood's Is it, then, of any interest to obtain a characterization and differentiation of the mental processes associated with different religious expressions in different religious groups? If we find it important to work out a phenomenology of religion, then a study of, say, the following kind would seem to be both an interesting and a neglected field: namely, to characterize the average emotive or conative processes evoked in the religious believer by the common religious expressions of his own religion,

[2] See Charles E. Osgood, George J. Suci, Percy H. Tannenbaum, *The Measurement of Meaning*, University of Illinois Press, Urbana 1957.

[3] Osgood, op. cit., p.7.

and to compare the result in different religions or religious factions; to compare the reactions to the language of one religion in the believers of that religion with the reactions to the same language in adherents to another religion or in secularized men, etc. We shall find later on that a psychological study along these lines is of importance for the solution of a widely discussed philosophical problem.

Description and explanation of metaphors   A brief glance at the category of religious expressions is enough to reveal that they are very often metaphorical or consist of indirect sentences. By means of an empirical inquiry, I think we could easily show that it is impossible to reformulate some of these metaphorical or indirect sentences in non-metaphorical or direct sentences, without altering their expressive power. Why this is the case can be explained by such theories as the interaction theory or the theory of circumstantial metaphors, or even by some symptom theory. Especially in aesthetic theory, there are many more aspects to the function of metaphors in non-cognitive sentences. We shall not enter into such a discussion, since this is a field in which the analysis of religious language seems to pose no special problems. One thing, however, needs to be stressed. In discussing religious statements, we pointed to a use of sentences which we termed situation-creating. Such a use seems to be of great importance for the expression of specific religious emotive and conative states. To express a certain emotion, religious men sometimes use a set of sentences which if seen as isolated sentences express nothing particular, but which together create a situation in which the emotion occurs and can be recognized. The sentences of a prayer can be analysed individually as statements, prescriptions and expressions of different kinds, but this is in some cases an unsatisfactory analysis. Their meaning is determined by the fact that they together constitute a situation of adoration. This situation is such that religious men find in it a specific emotion impossible to express in a single expression. Against this background, we can understand the importance of liturgy in almost all religions. What is said here and on p.54 can also explain why liturgical formulas in dead languages can be meaningfully used in the cultus, even by those who cannot speak or understand the language.[4]

(*iii*) *Finding the anchorage of the different expressions*   (iii) There are other empirical questions besides those of a psychological nature which need to be raised concerning the religious expressions used by religious men. Expressions, like statements, have an anchorage. In uttering a religious expression, religious men often suppose something as being the case in the real world or in a world of fantasy. An important empirical question is then: What anchorage do the different religious expressions used by religious men have?

Reappearance of the problems raised in Chapter II   Let us take as an example the following: 'Almighty God, Father of all mercies, we thine unworthy servants do give thee most humble and hearty thanks for all thy goodness and loving kindness to us, and to all men.' A Christian using this sentence in a prayer can be said to express an attitude of thankfulness, but this is a poor description of the speech-act. We must first add that it is probably an attitude of thankfulness *towards God*. In this case God is part of the anchorage of the sentence. We can go on to say that the sentence expresses an emotion of humility and, at the same time, has its anchorage in a certain relation between God and man. This anchorage belongs, according to most believers, to the real world; probably, however, many of them would refuse to use empirical methods to determine whether or not this anchorage really exists. It seems to be an empirical fact that many religious expressions localized in the real world have an anchorage which is such that the believers would refuse to use empirical methods to find out whether or not it actually exists in the real world. We can also suppose that there are religious expressions, the anchorage of which is in certain empirical facts. Some expressions surely have their anchorage

---

[4] The usage of old Church Slavonic in some Orthodox churches may perhaps provide a better example than the Latin of the Roman Catholic Church.

in a fictitious world: 'Oh, blessed is that land of God, Where saints abide for ever; Where golden fields spread far and broad, Where flows the crystal river. . . .'

B. The need of constructive theories   If the anchorage of a certain expression does not exist in the world where it is located, then the expression is out of order. This simple semantical observation leads us to a question which we cannot answer without making some philosophical decisions. Is the use of religious expressions a correct use of language or are some of these expressions out of order? If we accept the minimum thesis of empiricism, the answer must be that a religious expression, if it has an anchorage in the real world which it is impossible to investigate empirically, cannot be used correctly. We have seen that certain epistemological standpoints have led philosophers to suggest constructive theories of religious language which deny the existence of statements of the problematic set in a correct religious language. These epistemological standpoints ought, as a consequence, to lead the same philosophers to demand a revision of the use of religious expressions, e.g. expressions of thankfulness towards God. This means that an interpretation of premise (ii) in the argument on p.32 which leads to the conclusion (iv), has great consequences for the view taken of religious expressions. Is it, then, possible to achieve a revision of religious expressions which makes it reasonable to use them and at the same time to adhere to the minimum thesis of empiricism?

The non-cognitivist's solution   The easiest revision is to alter their localization in accordance with the following rule. If the anchorage, or part of the anchorage, of a religious expression is not an empirical state of affairs, then this anchorage ought not to be seen as anything belonging to the real world; i.e., the expression should be seen as an expression with a fictitious localization, or with a fictitious localization in a weak sense. It can in such a case be used as an indirect expression. It may seem superfluous to point to the consequences of a non-cognitive constructive theory in the field of religious expressions. It is seldom done. However, the elucidation of this point leads us to a neglected field of research which must be of great importance to those wishing to use a religious language in a non-cognitive interpretation. We shall call it 'the empirical challenge to the non-cognitivist'.

The empirical challenge to the non-cognitivist In Chapter II we encountered serious attempts to reduce many religious key-sentences belonging to the problematic set to expressions. According to Braithwaite, for instance, they are indirect expressions by virtue of being statements with a fictitious localization – i.e. 'stories'. The argument for this view contains, as mentioned above, a premise which requires a revised use of religious expressions. A consistent non-cognitive theory of religion is therefore not one that simply reduces certain problematic statements to religious expressions, but one involving a reduction to a revised form of religious expressions. Will, then, such revised expressions express the same emotive or conative impulses as they do among ordinary religious men? This is denied by some of those who have argued against the non-cognitive theories.[5] They have claimed that a religious language, interpreted according to Braithwaite's suggestions, no longer expresses the desire to live an agapaistic life. Against the background of our previous discussion, we can now see that this fundamental problem for a non-cognitive constructive theory of religious language can be solved empirically. We have seen that it might be possible to extend a semantic differential technique to the realm of religious sentences. It could then be tested whether or not a sentence expresses the same attitude for those believing the anchorage of the sentence to be a real state of affairs as for those who think it to be fictitious.

Charles L. Stevenson, in his well-known analysis of ethical

[5] For example A. C. Ewing, 'Awareness of God', *Philosophy* XL, 1965, p.13. Cf. Ninian Smart, who writes: 'The particular kind of marvelling involved in worship is linked to a doctrinal scheme and it is not possible properly to understand many of the propositions employed in praise without acquaintance with the scheme' (*Reasons and Faiths*, p.33). The question is very important for such theologians as Paul van Buren and his followers.

language, argues from the assumption that a certain 'emotive meaning' of a word can remain even when the 'descriptive meaning' is altered.[6] A reinterpretation of a religious expression which involves altering its localization exemplifies a process analogous to a change in the 'descriptive meaning' of the expression. Stevenson's theory of the independent 'emotive meaning' affords, if correct, some evidence for the hypothesis that religious expressions retain their expressive power after a revision of their anchorage. However, Stevenson's theory is not beyond dispute,[7] and it does not allow us to draw any consequences as to the long-term result of altering the localization of religious expressions. The sentence quoted above ('Almighty God . . . we . . . give thee most humble and hearty thanks . . .'). might now, in a European country, be a way of expressing a certain feeling of thankfulness even for a man who believes God to be a fantasy figure like Father Christmas. If, however, metaphysical Christian beliefs are absolutely dead in a society, then it seems improbable that expressions like this could have any function whatever. This is only a guess, but what is obvious is that a constructive theory of religious language, by which some religious sentences could be used as expressions, has to demonstrate by an empirical investigation that the sentences concerned really can have this function as a part of the revised language.

2. Expressions ascribed to God or to supernatural beings

The possibility of using empirical methods in the analysis   Many religious texts contain direct quotations of sayings of God. Often a prophet speaks the word of God, as in the Bible or the Quran. Among the sentences ascribed to God, it is easy to

[6] Charles L. Stevenson, *Ethics and Language*, Yale University Press, New Haven 1944, pp.72ff.

[7] For another view see the discussion between R. B. Brandt and C. L. Stevenson in *The Philosophical Review* LIX, 1950, and Axel Gyllenkrok, *Systematisk teologi och vetenskaplig metod med särskild hänsyn till etiken* (Systematic Theology and Scientific Method with Particular Reference to Ethics), Acta Universitatis Upsaliensis, Uppsala 1959, pp.68ff.

find some that are apparently expressions. 'Ah, I will vent my wrath on my enemies, and avenge myself on my face' (Isa. 1.24). We can hardly offer any successful psychological study of the emotions and will of the persons to which such sentences are ascribed. We are in the same predicament when we encounter songs of praise by angels and similar beings. However, the function of such sentences when used by religious men is worth noting.

It is obvious that the quotation of the expressions of God by a prophet is a means of expressing warning or encouragement. When these sentences are read nowadays, as part of a holy scripture, they probably communicate different emotions which can be studied in the same way as suggested for other expressions.

Concerning the anchorage of this kind of expression, we have to distinguish between three cases.

(i)   An anchorage of the expression is that a God with certain emotions exists in the real world.

(ii) An anchorage of the expression is that there is a God in the real world, but that the emotional reactions of God are fictitious.

(iii) All kinds of supernatural anchorage of the sentences are fictitious.

Probably, such sentences are workable expressions with all three kinds of anchorage. An atheist can read Isaiah's quotations of God as a piece of great poetry, and take the expressions ascribed to God as indirect expressions. In analogy to what was said in the former section, we can presume that the emotive meaning changes with a change of anchorage.

An empirical study of the anchorage of these sentences among religious men will surely reveal the importance of the distinction between (i) and (ii). (i) is the more common, but for some Christians at least, the use of an expression with an anchorage according to (i) would be an intolerable anthropomorphism. We consequently find, in theology, serious attempts to protect the use of religious expressions by God against an interpretation according to (i). The clearest theory is to be found in St Thomas, who introduces certain restrictions for the terms that can be analogically applied to God. Without such restrictions, our talk of God would lead to anthropomorphism. In order to be applicable to God analogically the terms must denote what he calls a simple perfection. A term denoting an emotion does not denote a simple perfection, and we cannot therefore talk or think about anything analogous to emotions in God.[8] St Thomas's theory can be seen as a constructive one, which takes up an interpretation current among some Christians and affords theological evidence for correcting the common use according to this interpretation. The theory is dependent upon certain assumptions of the Aristotelian and Neo-Platonic view of the world and, as far as I know, no modern reinterpretation of the theory of analogy has provided clear criteria which make an interpretation according to (i) impossible. However, I do believe that most modern theologians would reject (i). Persons adhering to the minimum thesis of empiricism or some similar theory would, of course, see any interpretation of such expressions other than (iii) as superstitious.

3. Sentences expressing a perspective

Questions raised by van Buren's theory   In his constructive theory of Christian language, Paul van Buren points to an important kind of sentence which he believes to express a certain way of seeing the world, history and oneself; this latter he terms a 'perspective'.[9] When a Christian assigns a position of central importance to Christ, he is expressing a perspective of history. This can be done by the sentence 'God raised up Jesus as Lord'. The historical perspective, according to van Buren, is the kernel of the Gospel.[10] A central thesis in his book is that perspective-sentences are non-cognitive, although they often have the form of statements. Van Buren's ideas bring into focus

---

[8] *C. Gent.* I, 30, *In I Sent.* 22, *De Veritate.* 1, 7, *S. Theol.* I, 13, 3 ad 1. Cf. Frederick Copleston, *Contemporary Philosophy*, The Newman Press, Westminster, Maryland 1956, p.37.

[9] Paul van Buren, *The Secular Meaning of the Gospel*, SCM Press, London 1963, p.156.   [10] Op. cit., p.193.

four questions of a kind which it is possible to answer, although van Buren himself makes no attempt to do so. (i) Is it possible that sentences like van Buren's perspective-sentences can function as non-cognitive expressions? (ii) Do religious men use certain religious sentences as non-cognitive perspective-expressions? (iii) Do religious men believe themselves to use certain sentences in this way? (iv) Are there any good philosophical or theological reasons for seeing some religious sentences as non-cognitive perspective-sentences?

Explanation of a possible non-cognitive usage The first question is important, and we can answer it by referring to our previous discussion. We pointed on p.45 to a kind of entity which we called ambiguous objects with a changing *Gestalt* (as distinct from ambiguous objects with an uncertain *Gestalt*). If we choose one possible *Gestalt* in preference to another, this is not a choice which can be justified by an appeal to facts. To express one way of seeing the object is not to make a statement which can be verified by scientific methods. One *Gestalt*, however, may fit a given person's evaluation better than another. To express this *Gestalt* is then a way of expressing the evaluation. Van Buren's perspective-sentences may be value-sentences of this kind. We can suppose the history of mankind to be an ambiguous object. To say something about the totality of history is to express one of the possible *Gestalts*, and thereby to express a kind of evaluation of history. If we also suppose all value-sentences to be non-cognitive, then we have a theory which explains how certain sentences like van Buren's example of perspective-sentences, which seem to be statements, can function as expressions. But, as noted above, if the ambiguous entity has an uncertain *Gestalt* and not a changing one, then sentences saying that one *Gestalt* is correct are statements. To claim that perspective-sentences are non-cognitive, we have to show that they relate to objects with a changing and not with an uncertain *Gestalt*. Van Buren, of course, has not proved this. He has not seen the problem.

An empirical problem of description Let us turn to the second question. Do religious men use sentences about Jesus as non-cognitive perspective-expressions? This is an empirical question, but it is difficult to answer. Probably we cannot say more than this: sentences which can be interpreted as non-cognitive perspective-expressions sometimes have, as their main function, the expression of values. The theory outlined above can then explain how it is possible for them to have this function. Sometimes, however, they are used by religious men as statements.

The third question is easily answered in the negative, and the fourth belongs to Chapter II. We shall not consider it further.

Summary   To sum up, we can say that van Buren, by pointing to perspective-sentences and claiming that they are non-cognitive, may have observed an important category of disguised expressions in religious language. Our theory of ambiguous objects with a changing *Gestalt* is an attempt to explain the machinery by which such expressions might work.

Our arguments here have been based on the premise that all value sentences, even moral ones, are non-cognitive. If they were cognitive, such perspective-sentences as express a moral evaluation would naturally be cognitive. The combination of analyses of religious language with different meta-ethical theories is a field which we now shall briefly discuss.

4. Examples of problems raised by an emotive theory of value

Definition of an emotive theory   The combination of theories of religious language with the various analytical theories relating to value-sentences brings to light a wide range of problems. The most problematical confrontation is probably with an emotive theory of value, and we shall restrict our discussion to this. A value-theory will be called emotive if it embraces the following two assumptions, which are logically independent of each other. (i) Values are no special category of entities in the world (an ontological assumption). (ii) The function of a sentence which makes it a value-sentence is that it expresses emotive states of mind (a semantical assumption). Most of the well-known emotive or non-cognitive value-theories involve these two assumptions.

Consequences for religious language If the emotive theory is correct, it has as a consequence that we must revise our understanding of religious language in at least two fields.

The first one is that of moral value-sentences ascribed to God, which constitute a fairly important set of religious sentences. In most religions God is thought of as expressing moral evaluations in regard to the behaviour of men and angels. If now the assumption of a moralizing activity on the part of God is combined with an emotive value-theory, then the conclusion must be that God has emotions. We have seen above that this is denied by many Christians. If they adhere to the emotive theory, they must consequently either reject all sentences expressing a moral judgment by God or suggest an interpretation by which God's moral reactions are referred to a fictitious world.

Many religious doctrines contain sentences stating a causal relation between a supernatural being and some moral state of affairs in the world: 'God has created the goodness of the universe and all the evil is due to the Devil.' Such doctrines, which are seen as central by many religious men, are difficult to interpret as meaningful from the standpoint of an emotive value-theory, since there are no moral properties of the world which can be causally dependent upon supernatural activities.

5. Additional questions concerning religious prescriptions

Remarks on constructive theories of prescriptions Prescriptions as well as expressions have an anchorage, and the analysis of religious expressions would lead to the same kind of problems as discussed above. We need add only that an attempt to revise the interpretation of religious prescriptions, in order to make them compatible with the minimum thesis of empiricism or a similar theory, will often mean interpreting as an expression a sentence generally used as a prescription. This, for instance, is what an atheist must often do if he wants to find a meaning in the prescriptions made by supernatural beings.

Special analytical questions   There are certain special properties of prescriptions which may be worth investigating if one wishes to formulate a theory of religious language.

Terminology   Different prescriptions are obeyed to different degrees. We are sometimes willing to comply with a prescription because we find that there are good *reasons* for doing so. However, the effect of a prescription is not due exclusively to the reasons for or against the behaviour prescribed. There are also a number of other factors which causally determine our willingness to follow certain prescriptions: our personal relation to the man who prescribes, fear, a desire to please, etc. Let us call these traits in the communicative situation 'obedience-promoting factors'. We shall also say that the reasons for a prescribed behaviour, together with the obedience-promoting factors, give a prescription 'prescriptive power'.

(i) An empirical descriptive study of reasons   It is now open to empirical research to determine what reasons are accepted by religious men for following or not following different religious prescriptions. This investigation may take the form of very simple interview-questions, like the following directed to Muslims:

'Why do you think we should comply with the following prescription: "Whether one or both of your parents attain old age with thee; say not to them, 'Fie', neither chide them, but speak unto them words respectful . . ." (Sura 17.23)?' The reasons given by most religious groups would probably reveal rather complicated thoughts about different kinds of authority.

(ii) An empirical description and explanation of obedience-promoting factors   It is much more difficult to investigate the obedience-promoting factors. One famous theory which – if correct – would explain the tendency to comply with the prescriptions of God or those believed to speak in this name is Freud's theory of the Oedipus complex.

(i) and (ii) can lead to the observation and empirical study of an important kind of disagreement   A task of some interest, which could be performed once the above questions have been considered, would be to clarify another type of agreement and disagreement, which has seldom been observed. People often agree about the prescriptive power of certain religious prescriptions, such as the Ten Commandments, but disagree about the reasons or are influenced by very different obedience-promoting factors.

Persons recommending a revision of the average interpretation of religious statements for philosophical or theological reasons often approve of some of the moral prescriptions of a religion like Christianity or Islam, and think that these prescriptions should be used and obeyed. But the arguments for the revision of the interpretation of religious statements generally have as a consequence a revision of the reasons for the religious prescriptions, or of the obedience-promoting factors. A person using sentences of the problematic set as statements with their localization in the real world and another person who uses sentences of the problematic set as indirect expressions can agree as to the prescriptive power of one of the Ten Commandments, but they would probably disagree over the reasons.

Disagreement over the reasons but agreement about the prescriptive power can be due also to theological theories of other kinds than those discussed in our Chapter II. Christian and Muslim theologians have tried to interpret parts of biblical and Quranic ethics according to some philosophical system, e.g. that of Aristotle. That involves referring some prescriptions of God, such as the Ten Commandments, to a realm of ethics which could be acknowledged without any belief in the revelation of God through the scriptures.[11] What is being done here is to revise the reasons for the prescriptions, and we get groups of religious people who agree as to the prescriptive power of certain religious prescriptions but disagree over the reasons.

[11] Teachings similar to the theory of a 'natural law' constituting the ground floor of the religious ethical system can be found in such a Muslim philosopher as al-Fárábí. See Dwight M. Donaldson, *Studies in Muslim Ethics*, SPCK, London 1953, p.107.

The obedience-promoting factors peculiar to religion generally include some beliefs: beliefs, for instance, about the
properties of God. Many principles for the revision of religious
language imply that some of these beliefs are wrong. The obedience-promoting function of religion, in so far as it depends on
such beliefs, must then be considered as something negative.

It is possible that a person will consider some religious reasons
for a prescription satisfactory but will find that the obedience-
promoting factors peculiar to religion contain some super-
stititous belief. The most common situation, however, is that
the philosophical principles leading to a radical revision of the
interpretation of religious statements will lead also to a rejection
of the special obedience-promoting factors of religion, as well
as the reasons. In a western-pluralistic society it is common, I
think, for people to agree upon some moral prescriptions such
as the Ten Commandments but to disagree about the reasons
and to be influenced by different obedience-promoting factors.

(iii) Descriptive studies of power prescriptions   The language of
most religions contains kinds of prescription which do not
occur in everyday language. As an example, we can take the
words of Jesus to the paralytic in Matt. 9.6: 'Rise, take up your
bed and go home.' This utterance is believed by most Christians
to bring about a supernatural state of affairs: '. . . he rose and
went home'. This can happen because the words of Jesus have a
certain 'authority and power'. Let us use the term 'power
prescriptions' for those prescriptions which are thought of by
some religious men as causing supernatural processes when they
are uttered.[12] A process will here be called supernatural for a

---

[12] The power-prescriptions may be seen as a sub-class of what could be
called 'power-sentences'. Power-sentences are those sentences which,
according to some religious men, cause supernatural effects when the
sentences are used in a speech-act. Many Christian theologians seem to
think that every sentence in the Bible or in the New Testament or every
sentence which is uttered by Christ has some supernatural effects. Very
many Christian theologians would hardly deny that the sentences also have
the semantical traits we have discussed, and it seems to be fruitless to take
up a general discussion in the philosophy of religion of the theological theory
which makes most Christian sentences into power-sentences. This theological

certain person if, and only if, this person believes it impossible to explain the occurrence of the process with the help of empirical science or common sense. By this definition, a process can be supernatural for one person and natural for another.

The existence and frequency of power prescriptions in a religion can be determined by an ordinary investigation of the texts of the religion, and of the verbal behaviour of religious men. Some sentences are described in the texts as having, in certain situations, effects which are believed to be extraordinary, i.e. to be impossible to explain without taking into account powers which lie outside the realm of sense experience and the common course of nature.

All kinds of magic formulas are power prescriptions. Power prescriptions are of great importance in almost every religion, and they need not take the linguistic form generally used for prescriptions. When a priest at a Christian baptism, according to the rites of many churches, reads the Lord's Prayer over the child, this must sometimes be interpreted as the utterance of power prescriptions that are believed to have certain supernatural effects concerning the relation between the child and evil spirits, or concerning original sin. The language of the Bible certainly contains numerous power prescriptions. It might be of interest from the point of view of the phenomenology of religion to study and compare what different religions or the different factions of a religion hold to be necessary conditions for the making of power prescriptions.

(iv) Constructive tasks relating to power prescriptions For those persons who really believe that power prescriptions bring about a supernatural process, power prescriptions naturally have types of anchorage which will bring an analysis back to the general problems relating to religious statements.

For a person holding the minimum thesis of empiricism, the

---

theory may perhaps have had some influence in the tradition which led to Heidegger's view of poetic language and to the theory which we have interpreted as the theory of transcendental symptoms. For examples from other religions see F. J. Streng, *Emptiness*, p.114.

existence of power prescriptions must be an instance of the superstitions of mankind. We could, however, ask if it is possible, without denying the minimum thesis of empiricism, to interpret power prescriptions as a special set of sentences which sometimes have a reasonable use.

One possibility is to assume that power prescriptions have some uncommon but quite natural causal consequences. The magician, as well as Jesus, is supposed to cause uncommon psychological or psycho-somatic effects by precisely such sentences, which are interpreted by many persons in such a way as to be, in our terminology, power prescriptions. If this is the case, we have here another field of empirical research: What are the properties of the person speaking, the speech-act, and the person addressed, that cause such effects to be characterized by some people as supernatural? It will probably be found that the properties of the sentences are of little importance, and that we consequently have no reason from a scientific point of view to classify power prescriptions as a specific kind of sentence. The view that power prescriptions are a certain category of prescriptions will then be seen as stemming from superstitious beliefs as to the power of words.

It might now be maintained that Jesus and his apostles, or Mohammed, or some other person using power prescriptions, were themselves foreign to the distinction which made it possible for us to talk of power prescriptions. One could say that the distinction between natural and supernatural effects reflects a philosophical standpoint which prophets and apostles do not have. We could then go on to say that an interpretation of their words which makes it possible to talk of power prescriptions is no closer to their own view than one which is compatible with a scientific description of uncommon effects their words under certain conditions have. This, however, is scarcely true. Even if Jesus or Mohammed did not use the concept of the supernatural, they undoubtedly distinguished between ordinary events and those in which God was working more directly than in the general course of nature. This is sufficient reason to maintain that, in important religious texts, there was from the beginning a set of prescriptions corresponding to what we have here termed power prescriptions.

Concluding remarks to Chapter III   The analysis of religious expressions and prescriptions seems to involve many interesting questions, which are often neglected. We have tried to point to such questions, and we have discussed appropriate methods by which they might be answered. However, we have found that the problems which we left in Chapter II recur at many important points. Even in the field of religious language considered in this chapter, the position taken in the analysis of the problematic set of sentences will be of decisive importance for the outcome of the analysis.

IV

RELIGIOUS PERFORMATIVES

It is obvious that performative utterances are of great importance in religious languages, and many philosophers have identified and discussed religious performatives. One book on religious language has the religious performatives as its main theme, namely L. Bejerholm, G. Hornig, *Wort und Handlung*.[1]

Introduction Some writers who have touched upon the problem of religious performatives seem to think that the identification of a religious utterance as a performative in some way solves certain problems in religious language. How far this is true will be discussed in the final section 4 of this chapter. Such a discussion is impossible without an investigation of the methods that can be used in analysing religious performatives, or a reflection upon the sort of results that can be achieved. An investigation of this kind is made in our section 3. In preparation, we must first discuss correctness-conditions for performatives in general (section 1) and make some important distinctions between different kinds of religious performative (section 2).

The general discussion of performatives has concerned itself to some extent with the difficulties of obtaining a suitable definition of this set of sentences. We have adopted a position in this discussion by our definition on p.11, and will not com-

---

[1] Lars Bejerholm, Gottfried Hornig, *Wort und Handlung. Untersuchungen zur analytischen Religionsphilosophie*, Gütersloher Verlagshaus Gerd Mohn, Gütersloh 1966. Comments on performative uses of religious sentences can be found in the following books: *Faith and the Philosophers*, ed. John Hick, Macmillan, London 1964, p.44; W. A. Christian, *Meaning and Truth in Religion*, pp.129 and 133; *Talk of God*, p.2; *Process and Divinity*, pp.436 and 440; T. R. Miles, *Religion and the Scientific Outlook*, pp.185f.

ment on it further. What is said below is compatible with a number of alternative definitions. Some writers of religious performatives, however, use a very loose definition and this, of course, complicates the discussion of what sentences to recognize as performatives.[2]

1. Conditions for the correct use of a performative

By our terminology, a performative cannot be true or false. It can, however, be used correctly or incorrectly. We shall say that a performative is used correctly if the same sentence is true when used as an indicative statement. The truth of this statement is generally dependent upon certain social conventions being followed, and some other statements being true. These conditions for the correct use of a performative will be called the correctness-conditions of the performative. The social and other state of affairs which must exist if the correctness-criteria are to be fulfilled constitute the anchorage of the performative.

Let us imagine a linguistic philosopher with a bottle of champagne, a beverage of which he has already consumed rather too much. Coming out to his car he breaks the bottle over the bonnet, saying earnestly: 'I name this ship Queen Elizabeth.' He is then using a performative incorrectly because the correctness-conditions for this performative are (*a*) the convention that the person using this performative has a certain mandate, which he has not, and (*b*) that it is true that there is a ship present, which is not the case. The anchorage of the performative is the social convention by which linguistic philosophers are seldom entrusted with the naming of ships, and that it should also be a certain ship at a certain place and time.

[2] Bejerholm, Hornig write: 'Wortverbindungen, die angewandt werden können, um etwas zu *bewirken*, bezeichnen wir im folgenden als "performative" Wortverbindungen' (op. cit., p.19).

2. The classification of religious performatives

Examples Let us now take some well-known examples of sentences that can obviously be used as performatives in religious language:

(i)   I pronounce that they be man and wife together . . .
(ii) I baptize thee in the Name of the Father, and of the Son, and of the Holy Ghost.
(iii) I absolve thee from all thy sins . . .
(iv) And Jephthah made a vow unto the Lord and said, 'If thou wilt give the Ammonites into my hand, then whoever comes forth from the doors of my house to meet me, when I return victorious from the Ammonites, shall be the Lord's, and I will offer him up for a burnt offering' (Judg. 11.30).
(v)   God said: 'I establish my covenant with you, that never again shall all flesh be cut off by the waters of a flood . . .' (Gen. 9.13).

Let us discuss the correctness-conditions and anchorage of these performatives. We can thereby draw attention to a distinction which is relevant to the analysis – a distinction between two sets of performatives in religious language.

Unproblematic religious performatives When (i) is said by a priest to the bride and bridegroom in the church, both an atheist and a religious man can recognize it as a correct use of a performative. This agreement depends on the fact that the correctness-condition for this performative often does not involve the acceptance of any religious statement, or any special religious convention. You can deny that the priest has any special religious authority, and find his prayers and blessings ridiculous, but still accept that he has the legal mandate to declare people married. Many Christians – for example, Lutherans – also agree that no circumstances dependent upon the Christian revelation are necessary for a marriage to be created by a priest saying (i). Consequently, in the case of (i), there are situations in which the performative can function correctly according to both religious and non-religious men without any special religious supposition. We will call sentences like (i) in such a situation 'unproblematic religious performatives'.

Religious performatives with both an unproblematic and a problematic interpretation Let us now think of a priest who utters (ii) to a child, acting according to the ritual of baptism. Everyone must admit that he is uttering a performative, and people with a different theology and outlook on the world can agree that the performative is used correctly. It is really a true statement that the priest is baptizing. But is it possible for a religious man and an atheist who are in agreement as to the correctness of the use to agree also as to the correctness-conditions in this case? This is an empirical question, and the answer is that it is often impossible. An atheist may say that the acceptance of certain conventions concerning the solemn naming of a child is sufficient for us to be able to say that the priest baptizes in the situation described. But a religious man will generally add that the performative is misused if God does not in some way take account of what is done by uttering the performative. If this is not the case, he will say that the priest did not really perform a baptism in saying 'I baptize . . .'. This means that a religious man will add certain special correctness-conditions, which the atheist is not bound to accept.

It is also true that different religious persons have different ideas in regard to the content of these additional claims. This is well-known from the history of the Christian church. The additional correctness-conditions generally accepted by religious men include sentences which are candidates for the problematic set of sentences, for example sentences concerning actions of God. When the correctness-conditions of a performative involve sentences of the problematic set, we shall say that we have a 'problematic religious performative'. Our example (ii) is then a performative with both a problematic and an unproblematic interpretation.[3]

---

[3] From an empirical point of view, what I. Hedenius says about religious performatives in general is true for religious performatives like (ii): 'All that

Different problematic religious performatives   In their normal use, the remaining examples (iii)–(v) are, in different respects, problematic religious performatives. Believers and non-believers often agree that, if we refuse to accept sentences of the problematic set, then they have no correct use. A correct use of (iii) usually has as a premise that there is a God who has given to certain persons the authority to forgive sins. To use (iv) without believing in a God who accepts very special conventions in regard to promises seems to be senseless, and acceptance of the idea that God uses performatives generally requires at least the same suppositions as to believe that Jephthah really made a promise to God.

3. The analysis of religious performatives

The main analytical task for a philosopher of religion concerns the problematic religious performatives, including performatives like (ii). We shall indicate three approaches (I–III) to such an analysis.

I. An empirical study of correctness-conditions   It is possible to establish empirically and in detail the correctness-conditions and anchorage of certain religious performatives, relative to specific groups of religious men. The method is to ask, with the help of some suitable questionnaire, what requirements, according to believers, must be met for the indicative sentence (statement) corresponding to the performative to be held as true. In the case of (ii) we might ask, for instance, whether it can really be a baptism if the person saying 'I baptize . . .' is a layman. Most theologians would answer in the affirmative, but many Christian laymen would probably deny that a baptism had taken place in such a case. For the latter group it is then a correctness-condition for the performative 'I baptize . . .' that the person using it should be a priest. In a similar way, we could probably establish that in nearly all Christian

---

is wrong with them is that some people expect too much of them.' Ingemar Hedenius, 'Performatives', *Theoria* XXIX, 1963, p.125.

groups it is a correctness-condition for this performative that the person using it should himself be baptized. Can we perform a baptism if it is false that Jesus is the Son of God and that the Holy Spirit exists? Many Christians would deny this, and we have here the truth of a far-reaching theological theory as a correctness-condition. Analysing (iii) in a similar way, we can describe a whole spectrum of theological theories concerning the ministry.

Critical remarks on an analysis of performatives   In their discussion of religious performatives like (ii) and (iii), Bejerholm and Hornig have disregarded the fact that such performatives, when they function among religious men, have theological theories as correctness-conditions. Once we know that they are performatives, Bejerholm-Hornig seem to mean, we recognize also that the only condition for their correct use is that the ritual of the church is followed.[4] They seem to suggest that a major proportion of the theological controversies relating to the ministry can therefore be resolved by drawing attention to the performative character of sentences like (ii) and (iii). It is not, however, true that a religious believer, having noticed the performative character of sentences like (ii) and (iii), will agree that adherence to a certain liturgical behaviour is the only condition for a correct use of these sentences. As we have demonstrated, the old controversies come back as further correctness-conditions. If Bejerholm and Hornig are trying not to describe the factual use of religious performatives but to suggest a less problematical use, their analysis is more interesting. But the suggestion that we should accept certain liturgical rules as the only correctness-conditions for performatives like (ii) and (iii) will probably attract very little enthusiasm in religious circles. We will discuss below how far it is possible to solve philosophical problems by a new interpretation of religious performatives.

Special problems concerning examples (iv) and (v)   (iv) is a kind of performative that was of supreme importance in Old Testament

---

[4] Bejerholm, Hornig, op. cit., p.26.

days. As a consequence of the promise to God here quoted, Jephthah, according to the narrative given in Judges, had to sacrifice his only daughter. To make a promise to God seems to be a solemn act of a quite different order from promises between men. The correctness-conditions for such a performative can in principle be established by the same method as in our former example: in practice, of course, this is almost impossible since we cannot be sure that any religious men nowadays make promises of the same kind as Jephthah's. We must apply here the ordinary principles for the interpretation of historical texts. If we investigate, by comparing different documents, how a promise to God was conceived in Old Testament times, then we may conclude that it is impossible to make a promise in this sense unless God is supposed to be in the habit of punishing very severely those who fail to fulfil their promises to him. In another age, a promise to God may be regarded as something less dramatic, and religious men may find that no more needs to be supposed concerning God in order to make promises to God possible than that he should regularly entertain certain expectations and claims similar to human ones when a person says to him 'I promise . . .'

Performatives like (v) are fundamental to Christianity, but in this case the empirically-minded student of religion can expect nothing from a closer examination of the correctness-criteria. (Beliefs as to God's intentions and habits can naturally be studied empirically.)

The anchorage of the performatives so far discussed consists – apart from ordinary social conventions – of rules dependent upon God (e.g. those regulating baptism and absolution), non-empirical beings (e.g. God and the Holy Spirit) and acts and habits of God.

II. An empirical study of the localization In discussing religious expressions, we noted that some religious men think the ascription of emotions to God to imply a false anthropomorphism. We must now ask if the same is not true of the properties of God which constitute an anchorage of certain religious performatives.

This is also an empirical question. It can be answered by studying how religious men react to different statements about God. We may find that part of the anchorage of the problematic religious performatives does not, according to some Christians, belong to the real world, although they will find the performatives meaningful. There may be Christians who agree that certain habits of God and authorizations given by God are the anchorages of performatives like (iii) and (iv), but that they belong to a religious world of fantasy. If part of the anchorage of a performative is referred to a fictitious world, the performative will here be said to have a fictitious localization. The aim of analysis (II) of religious performatives is now to establish the localization of the performatives empirically. As yet an analysis of the localization of religious performatives in any living religion will probably not prove fruitful, since we can be fairly sure that religious men will find a performative either senseless or localized in the real world. However, it is of importance to notice this kind of analysis since, as we shall see, it is a consequence of some suggested reformations of religious language that performatives with a fictitious localization should become common.

III. Constructive theories   We have demonstrated in Chapter II how and why many philosophers think that sentences of the problematic set cannot be statements with a localization in the real world. A primary reason, we have seen, is that there is no method by which it can be shown whether or not the anchorage of such sentences exists. From what has been said about religious performatives in I and II, it now follows that those who deny for this reason the possibility that sentences of the problematic set are statements with a localization in the real world are bound to hold the view that the correctness-conditions for the problematic kind of religious performatives can seldom be fulfilled. This is the same as saying that religious men, when they use performatives of the problematic kind, are using the language incorrectly. They are behaving like the philosopher in our example who utters: 'I name this ship Queen Elizabeth.'

We can now ask if there is any reinterpretation of the problematic religious performatives which would make it possible to avoid these difficulties.

Finding and recommending an unproblematic use   We have shown that there are performatives which obviously have both a problematic and an unproblematic use. In the case of such performatives, we can easily avoid the problems by eliminating the problematic use from the religious language. It might also be possible to find an unproblematic use for some of the problematic performatives, and to prescribe this use as the correct one. This is perhaps possible in the case of our example (iii). We may find it reasonable that persons dealing professionally with the care of others should be entrusted with the authority to express vicarious forgiveness. It is not reasonable that everyone should do this; human relations would then become exceedingly entangled. But it is not absurd to adopt the social habit of giving this authority to persons who have some special experience of human reactions. We may think that it is necessary, in certain cases, for a person to be forgiven, and that it is impossible for him to obtain this forgiveness from the person whom he thinks he has wronged. If we now make this social habit common, and if we count priests among those with the authority to forgive vicariously, then there is an unproblematic correct use of the performative (iii) as uttered by a priest. This use, we can then claim, is the proper use of such religious performatives. There are many non-Christian persons today who find the custom of going to confession very important from the standpoint of mental hygiene. These persons have perhaps begun to reinterpret the performative (iii) along the lines here suggested. The method of solving the problem of religious performatives now discussed will be referred to as 'finding and recommending an unproblematic use'.

Altering the localization   It is possible to invent an unproblematic use for many religious performatives. A promise to God can be seen as the reinforcement of an ordinary promise, etc. Undoubtedly, however, many performatives analogous to (iv) must be seen as quite unnecessary sentences when used as unproblematic performatives. (v), of course, can never be reinterpreted by finding and recommending an unproblematic use. We must here try to find another way of giving problematic performatives an unproblematical use in religious language. Let us try the method of 'altering the localization'. To alter the localization of a performative means in this case to refer its anchorage to a fictitious world. The meaning of this can be seen most clearly in the case of (v). God and his social and linguistic habits exist only in an imagined world. The whole anchorage (with the exception of human beings) is thought of as not belonging to the real world. We shall say in this case that the performative has a fictitious localization in a strong sense. Can such performatives be of any use in our language? This will depend on the attitude we adopt to the role of indirect statements and expressions, which we have discussed above. The only meaningful use of a performative with a fictitious localization in a strong sense seems to be as part of a story, which as a whole constitutes one or many indirect statements or expressions. As suggested in our first chapter, it seems impossible to speak of sentences which are performatives in a fictitious world and at the same time have a performative function in the real world.

In the case of (iii) and (iv) we can conceivably alter parts of the anchorage so that some will belong to a fictitious world (God, his commands, his ethical code, etc.), and others to the real world (social conventions concerning forgiveness, promising, etc.). We will then speak of a performative with a fictitious localization in a weak sense. If such sentences have any performative function at all in the real world, it would seem necessary to interpret them along the lines here referred to as 'finding and recommending an unproblematic use'. The idea that there is a God in some fictitious world is of no importance to the performative function unless we introduce the habit of seeing these ideas, when associated with a performative, as strengthening the performative force. There is also another possible interpretation of sentences like (iv) which are part of a narrative with a fictitious localization. The performative sentences can then, together with other sentences, be indirect statements or expressions, i.e. we can interpret performatives with a fictitious localization in a weak sense in the same way as those with a fictitious localization in a strong sense.

4. *The gain in identifying and analysing performatives in religious language*

We are now ready to discuss what can be gained in clarity about a religious language by identifying and analysing its performative elements.

To classify a sentence as a performative can be either a descriptive or a constructive proposal The first thing to note is that the mere classification of a sentence as a performative can be either a descriptive or a constructive task. In order to know if a philosopher is right when he says that a certain sentence is a performative, we must know whether he wants to describe an existing use of the sentence among a certain group of believers or to prescribe a new and better use of the sentence.

The result will depend on the choice of analytical method Secondly, the outcome of an analysis of these factual or desired performatives will depend on the analytical methods described in our former section. I and II are relevant only when we have found a factual performative use of a sentence; a constructive task can always be performed along the alternative lines presented under III.

Let us concentrate our discussion upon two important examples of sentences which are classified as performatives by different authors, but which are not obviously sentences of this kind.

An analysis of 'I believe in God . . .' as a performative In his contribution to *Talk of God*, N. H. G. Robinson writes: 'When, for example, the religious believer declares "I believe in God the Father Almighty" or "We acknowledge Thee to be the Lord", it is clear that whatever he is doing he is not simply giving assent to a proposition. His words have something of a performative character . . .'[5] We will limit our discussion to his first example. Can the sentence 'I believe in God' be a performative? Robinson notes the differences between such a sentence and sentences which are obviously performatives. He still thinks that we create a new state of affairs when we utter such sentences as 'I believe . . .' 'In an epistemological sense, or perhaps more accurately, in a responsive sense, they do make him God who ontologically was already God.'[6] This seems to be an interpretation of 'I believe . . .' similar to the performative analysis of 'I know . . .' suggested by J. L. Austin.[7] In his influential essay 'Other Minds', Austin argues that the phrase 'I know . . .' has a performative function: What I do when I say 'I know that S is P' is that *I give others my word* for saying that S is P. This observation, according to Austin, eliminates certain traditional problems concerning the nature of knowledge. However, the performative analysis of 'I know . . .' suffers from a certain weakness which the performative analysis of 'I believe in God' seems to share; Robinson also gives the impression of being aware of this. If it is to be possible to call these sentences performatives, then we must accept a very wide definition of the term, and this wide definition makes the classification of a sentence as a performative less interesting. This kind of critique of Austin has been expressed very clearly by R. M. Chisholm.[8] His definition of 'performative in a strict sense' coincides with the definition of performatives adopted here. Chisholm points out that sentences like 'I know . . .' are not performatives in this sense. He acknowledges, however, that sentences like 'I know . . .' and 'I believe . . .' can have a performative function in an extended sense.[9] To note this is important, but by no

---

[5] N. H. G. Robinson in *Talk of God*, p.2. Cf. ibid. p.vii.

[6] *Talk of God*, p.2.

[7] J. L. Austin, 'Other Minds', *Proceedings of the Aristotelian Society*, Suppl. Vol XX, Harrison and Sons, Ltd., London 1946, pp.170ff.

[8] R. M. Chisholm, *Theory of Knowledge*, pp.15–18.

[9] Chisholm, op. cit., pp.16ff. In discussing the sentence 'I believe . . .', Chisholm thinks of it in contexts other than religious ones. What he says about the function of the phrase can, however, easily be transferred to its use in the creed, where the phrase of course does not indicate any doubt.

means so far-reaching as their classification as performatives according to our definition, or according to Chisholm's definition of a performative in a strict sense.

What, then, does this extended sense of performative mean? Chisholm seems to have in mind the following definition: that a sentence is a performative in an extended sense means that the sentence is sometimes used as a synonym for a strict performative. We shall adopt this terminology. Thus the sentence 'I know' sometimes means the same as 'I guarantee . . .'. We must now ask whether there are any performative synonyms to the use of 'I believe . . .' in any religious context. This question is taken up, from another starting point, by Bejerholm and Hornig. They say that the sentence 'I believe in God' in some religious situations is an elliptic way of saying, for example:

I confess: I believe in God.
I declare: I believe in God.
I promise: I believe in God.[10]

These sentences can be performatives according to our definition, and it is a plausible empirical hypothesis that 'I believe in God' is sometimes used as a synonym for these performatives.

It is of analytical interest to note this interpretation of 'I believe', but it does not, of course, solve any problems concerning religious belief, since I must know what 'I believe in God' means as a statement for the performatives exemplified above to have any meaning. Even if there is a use of 'I believe . . .' as an extended performative of another kind than in the examples of Bejerholm and Hornig, there remains a non-performative use of 'I believe . . .', the analysis of which involves many problems. – To analyse further the performatives formulated by Bejerholm and Hornig would be of little importance for the analysis of religious language, since they are all performatives of the unproblematic kind.

An analysis of 'This is my body' as a performative   An original proposal as candidate for the set of religious performatives is

---

[10] Bejerholm, Hornig, op. cit., p.50.

made by Bejerholm and Hornig. They think that the sentence
'This is my body' can be interpreted as a performative when
used as a key-sentence in the Christian celebration of the
eucharist.[11] It is not clear whether the authors mean that the
sentence has *de facto* a performative use, or that it can be given
such a use as a reformation of religious language. They probably
think that it is sometimes used as a performative and that this
use is less difficult than other common uses of the sentence.[12]

What does it mean to interpret 'This is my body' as a performative? The answer given by Bejerholm and Hornig is as
follows.[13] Liturgy is regulated by certain rules comparable to
the rules regulating marriage in society. To use the performative 'I pronounce that they be man and wife together' is to give
two persons a new status in social intercourse. They are a
married couple. In an analogous way the uttering of 'This is
my body' could be an act which changes the role of the bread
in the liturgy. By uttering the sentence, and only by this act,
the priest gives the bread the function of the body of Christ in
the liturgical drama. It becomes the body of Christ.

Thus far their reasoning seems correct. This is a possible
interpretation of the formula which probably has this meaning
for some Christians. Bejerholm and Hornig, however, believe
that the performative interpretation makes the formula less
problematic than an interpretation of it as a power prescription,
and here their argument is unsatisfactory.[14] The act performed
by uttering 'This is my body' has been interpreted in various
ontological ways in the Christian traditions. We have different
well-known dogmatic explanations of the supposed fact that
the bread in the eucharist is the body of Christ. Bejerholm
and Hornig now argue that we can avoid this controversy in
Christian theology if we achieve the semantic insight that the
sentence 'This is my body' is a performative. It is then possible,
they think, to say that the bread really is the body of Christ

[11] Bejerholm, Hornig, op. cit., p.98.
[12] Cf. Bejerholm, Hornig, op. cit., p.106.
[13] Bejerholm, Hornig, op. cit., pp.100ff.
[14] Bejerholm, Hornig, op. cit., pp.102ff. Cf. ibid., p. 112.

subsequent to the utterance of the words of institution without making any ontological suppositions. Bejerholm and Hornig do not claim that most Christians would make such an interpretation. The authors are also open to the possibility of making a traditional ontological description of the act of consecration, even if the words of institution are interpreted as performatives. Their aim here is to offer an interpretation of the performatives which is easier to accept from a philosophical point of view, and which could be accepted also by Christians. This means that they seem to be attempting an analysis of the performative use of the words of institution in accordance with line (III) in section 2 above. They do not, however, complete their argument. This must be done in accordance with one of the lines indicated in (III) [pp.95ff.]. The first line is to find and recommend an unproblematic use. Is it reasonable to try to point out and recommend an unproblematic use of the performative 'This is my body'? Hardly. It is difficult to interpret the rules governing a Christian service in such a way that they can be accepted without the assertion of a statement of the problematic set. They generally involve certain suppositions about the acts of God towards men. The radical secular reinterpretation of a Christian service by van Buren and others may perhaps offer an opportunity to interpret the performative unproblematically,[15] but it is very difficult to imagine any reasonable conventions analogous to those for marriage or the solemn naming of a child, according to which certain persons in certain circumstances could declare bread to have a role called the body of Christ. A secular interpretation is easier if we follow the second possibility and alter the localization of the performative. The celebration of the eucharist can then be seen as a fictitious drama in which the performative has a function. This drama can, as a whole, reveal something important about the world – for example, a perspective in the meaning discussed above. This is a theory similar to van Buren's. But this kind of unproblematic interpretation of the sentence 'This is my body' is not due in any way to the per-

[15] Van Buren, op. cit., pp.183ff.

formative interpretation. We can achieve the same secularization of a power prescription by localizing it in a fictitious world. The conclusion is that Bejerholm and Hornig have made an important observation concerning the interpretation of an important liturgical formula, but that their interpretation can hardly solve any of the traditional theological or philosophical problems connected with the use of the sentence.

An interpretation of power prescriptions as performatives   Bejerholm-Hornig's analysis raises the question whether some of the sentences which are often regarded as power prescriptions cannot be interpreted as performatives. I think it is seldom the case that a religious sentence is seen by some religious believers as a power prescription and by other believers, or in other circumstances, as a performative. However, it might be possible to suggest, as a reformation of religious language, that power prescriptions should if possible be interpreted as performatives.

If this suggestion is to solve any fundamental problems, then the performative must be of the unproblematical kind. Let us try to provide an example of such an interpretation. When Jesus says to the leper in Matt. 8.4 'I will; be clean', this is obviously seen by the evangelist as a power prescription. In a performative interpretation it would mean that Jesus, by his words, altered the isolated social situation of the leper. The sentence is then equivalent to a sentence of the following kind: 'I hereby declare that you are an ordinary member of the social community.' Such a radical reinterpretation of religious language, however, would seem to make it rather uninteresting to many people. For those, however, who wish to avoid the epistemological problems involved in the use of religious language and still believe that this language is capable of expressing something important, it seems a better way to alter the localization of problematic sentences, including both power prescriptions and problematic performatives.

Summary   We have seen in this chapter that it is important to notice the performative function of religious sentences. The mere recognition of this function can solve some puzzling problems concerning the function of religious language. A classification of performatives in accordance with our suggestions in section 2 can furnish the starting-point of an analysis which, in accordance with line I or II in section 3, can reveal important and neglected traits in the function of a religion. Such an analysis is an empirical task, and it belongs to the phenomenology of religion. The approaches suggested in section 3 III for finding an unproblematic use for the problematical performatives can in certain cases lead to the recognition of a reasonable and unproblematical use of a sentence generally used as a problematical performative. Often, however, it will bring us back to the problems observed in Chapter II. Against this background, we have illustrated in our final section the fact that it is of importance to observe sentences which have a neglected *de facto* performative use and to point out possible performative reinterpretations of certain sentences. This, however, must be followed by an analysis according to I, II or III in section 3; it thereby becomes obvious that the interpretation of a religious sentence as a performative fails to offer any revolutionary insights. Summing up this chapter, we are bound to observe that the fundamental problems of religious language cannot be solved by observing its performative use. On the contrary, they are underlined.

V

THE EPISTEMOLOGICAL BASIS

Summary We have seen in Chapters II–IV that the common theories of religious language consist, often, of descriptive theories interwoven with other kinds of approach. We have tried to uncover these descriptive tendencies and indicate the empirical methods by which we can acquire knowledge in this field. We have formulated certain hypotheses which it may be reasonable to believe to be true. In our evaluation, a descriptive study of religious language is an important and fruitful task for scholarship, provided one is willing to face the more intricate questions in the field.[1]

We have noticed, however, at almost every stage of our discussion of the different kinds of religious sentence, that the important crossroads in theories of religious language are the different interpretations given to certain confusing key-sentences which we have labelled the 'problematic set of sentences'. We have seen that present-day religious language is most likely to contain such sentences, and that they are used as statements with a localization in the real world.

Many philosophers find such statements false or theoretically meaningless. They have therefore tried to find traits in the religious language concerned which will make it possible to use the language in a reasonable way without making statements of the problematic set. Such very thorough reconstructions of religious language involve numerous difficulties. We have pointed out some of these difficulties (for example, the empirical challenge to the non-cognitivist), and we have seen that they

[1] Cf. Bochenski, *The Logic of Religion*, pp.14 and 42.

are not restricted to the revision of those parts of the language which seem to be used as statements by religious men. If, however, it really is true that sentences of the problematic set cannot be statements with a localization in the real world, then a philosophy of religious language which aims to make their use reasonable has no choice but to try to overcome the difficulties.

Some of the most influential constructive theories examined above (for example Bultmann's and Tillich's) have been shown to be suggestive of an interpretation of religious language which erases such sentences as are obviously false, and which also tries to explain how most of the sentences of the problematic set can be used to express some kind of cognition concerning the real world. Underlying these theories, however, we found the acceptance of at least one sentence of the problematic set that is a statement with its localization in the real world, and which cannot be explained by these theories. It has also emerged that these theories therefore ascribe knowledge-claims to religion which go beyond scientific knowledge. If we are to contemplate accepting such a view of religious language, we must show independently of these theories that it can be reasonable to use sentences of the problematic set as statements with their localization in the real world, and further that some theoretical gain is involved in the reduction of reinterpretation of these sentences as suggested by the theory.

The key-question   We are now about to discuss the key-question whether it is reasonable to use some sentences of the problematic set as statements with a localization in the real world. It is here convenient to look again at the simple but important argument given on p.32. It is clear that we can avoid the conclusion only if we can indicate a method for determining whether or not the anchorage of these sentences exists in the real world. It is also evident that acceptance of this method must involve a refutation of the minimum thesis of empiricism, or at least an addition to it. We shall begin by discussing various methods suggested by philosophers of religion.

1. Eschatological Verification

The argument First a few words about what is called the theory of eschatological verification. This theory has appeared in the literature in several forms. A clear formulation, illustrated by an ingenious parable, is given by J. Hick.[2] The theory says that there are statements which will be verified only in another life, if there is such a life. Such statements belong to the problematic set in the perspective of this life and they are impossible to verify or falsify; since, however, we know – if we broaden our view – a method by which we can verify them in principle, they are statements with their localization in the real world. The adherents of this theory thus think that some religious sentences of the problematic set are open to eschatological verification, and that they are therefore statements.

Critical remarks Two comments must be made on this theory. The first is that it is uninteresting; the second is that it is question-begging. What makes it uninteresting is its *ad hoc* character. Given any set of apparently nonsensical sentences compatible with the idea of a life after death, you could argue – by appealing to the idea of eschatological verification – that they are statements with their localization in the real world. The appeal to eschatological verification begs the question because it allows us to see problematic religious sentences as statements only if the sentence 'There is a life after death', is a statement with its localization in the real world, and this sentence, if any, itself belongs to the problematic set of religious sentences.[3]

2. Religious Experience

As a second attempt to find a method by which a sentence of

[2] John Hick, *Philosophy of Religion*, Prentice-Hall, Inc., Englewood Cliffs, N. J. 1963, pp.101f. Cf. I. M. Crombie, 'The Possibility of Theological Statements', in *Faith and Logic*, ed. Basil Mitchell, George Allen and Unwin, London 1957, p.76.

[3] Cf. Blackstone, *The Problem of Religious Knowledge*, pp.122f.

the problematic set might be shown to have an anchorage in
the real world, we shall note the family of theories which sees a
method of justifying certain knowledge-claims in religious or
mystical experience. It would take too much space to summarize here all the arguments and counter-arguments concerning religious experience that have been offered in the
modern debate.[4] Instead, we shall first try to formulate one of
the strongest arguments given in the relevant literature against
the view that religious experience could yield any knowledge
of the anchorage of problematic religious sentences.[5] We shall
then discuss whether any of the theories of religious knowledge
escape this argument.

An argument against the knowledge-claims of religious experiences   We
will call the kind of experiences concerned 'extraordinary
experiences'. Every such experience of something existing that
is not a sense-experience of the kind we rely on in our everyday

[4] Asking if there is some kind of knowledge given through religious
experiences, one can have in mind two different questions. The first one is
whether religious experiences can cause certain theories which later ordinary
scientific testing can demonstrate as true or probable. The second question
is whether certain assertions about reality can be based exclusively upon
religious experiences. In the first case the question concerns the heuristic
importance of the religious experiences: in the second case they are ques-
tioned as verifying processes. Our discussion is restricted to the second case. –
Examples of books favourable to knowledge-claims based on religious
experiences are John Baillie, *Our Knowledge of God*, Oxford University
Press, London 1939; Herbert H. Farmer, *Towards Belief in God*, SCM
Press, London 1942; John Wilson, *Language and Christian Belief*, Macmillan,
London 1958. Interesting critical commentaries to Baillie's and Farmer's
books are given by C. B. Martin in his article 'A Religious Way of Knowing',
Mind LXI, 1959, pp.497–512. Kai Nielsen has criticized Wilson's arguments in 'Christian Positivism and the Appeal to Religious Experience',
The Journal of Religion XLII, 1962, pp.248–61. Many common arguments
against intuitive cognition of God are discussed and refuted by A. C. Ewing
in his article 'Awareness of God', *Philosophy* XL, 1965, pp.1–17. Among the
many critical analyses of arguments for the existence of God based on direct
experiences of God we could also mention two chapters (III and IV) in
R. W. Hepburn's *Christianity and Paradox*; Hepburn's analyses are concen-
trated on Martin Buber.

[5] An argument of this kind is formulated by Alasdair MacIntyre in his
Difficulties in Christian Belief, SCM Press, London 1959, pp.7of. Cf. A. Flew,
God and Philosophy, pp.131f.

life or appeal to in science is an extraordinary experience. We can now formulate a possible argument against the knowledge-claims of religious experiences. It is not a formal and precise formulation, but it is enough to illustrate one of the greatest difficulties in appealing to religious experience.

(i)   There are people who have had strong and extraordinary experiences of seeing or meeting something real, and these experiences have obviously not been related to anything outside the persons concerned. They have, in fact, been illusions.

(ii) Those claiming to have a knowledge of something outside their own persons as a result of extraordinary experiences are therefore bound to offer some method by which one can discriminate between knowledge and illusion.

(iii) The method offered does not work.

(iv) We cannot base any knowledge-claims concerning the external world exclusively upon extraordinary experiences.

The two first steps (i) and (ii) seem unavoidable. A person believing in extraordinary experiences as a way of acquiring knowledge cannot deny that there are a great number of erroneous extraordinary experiences – meetings with ghosts, demons, devils, angels, saints and gods – and he must discriminate between different kinds of experience in accordance with (ii). If (iii) is true, then conclusion (iv) is undoubtedly justified.

General difficulties in meeting the argument   The important question is, then, whether anyone has provided, or can provide, any workable criteria for discriminating between extraordinary experiences of something real and illusory ones.[6]

Unfortunately, the existing theories seem to provide no clear criteria. Without excluding the possibility of their being given in the future, we will now turn to another line of thought which has been the focus of many debates and which seems to be a

[6] For a discussion see Ninian Smart, 'Interpretation and Mystical Experience', *Religious Studies* 1, 1965, pp.75–87. Note the quotation from Zaehner on p.86.

more fruitful attempt to meet the argument against knowledge
by religious experience.

A line of reasoning which avoids the main difficulties   Many theologians and philosophers have claimed that there is a very sharp
border-line between illusory extraordinary experiences and
extraordinary experiences of something real. This border-line,
however, cannot be described to persons who have not had a
genuine experience. It is therefore vain to try to formulate any
criteria discriminating between different extraordinary experiences. As soon as a person has had the kind of extraordinary
experience which yields knowledge, he will see the immense
difference between such experiences and those that are illusory.
In other words, the genuine extraordinary experience is self-
authenticating. What the philosopher can do is to point out the
circumstances in which the self-authenticating experience occurs.

An example of a theory which follows this last line of thought
is a theology based on a personal encounter with God, analogous to the specific I-Thou relation between men. Martin
Buber is the best-known name in this tradition.[7] The great
mystics who hold their experiences to be indescribable are on
the same line.[8] Let us look a little more closely at this line of
thought, as stated by a philosopher aware of the kind of
problems here discussed, H. H. Price.[9]

[7] See Martin Buber, *I and Thou*, Edinburgh 1937, It is, however, doubtful
whether Buber's theory is intended to be a basis for any kind of *statement*
about the person encountered. Cf. Virgil C. Aldrich, 'Tinkling Symbols', in
Faith and the Philosophers, ed. John Hick, Macmillan, London 1964, pp.49ff.
Aldrich has provided a short but interesting interpretation of similar theories
and confronted the theories with the observations of the use of 'you' made by
linguistic philosophers. His interpretation seems to exclude the 'I–Thou
philosophy' being seen as a theory which supports the legitimacy of using
sentences of the problematic set as statements. The I–Thou theory embraces,
however, a kind of metaphysics.

[8] See W. T. Stace, *Religion and the Modern Mind*, J. B. Lippincott Company,
Philadelphia and New York 1952, p.229. It is important to note that some
great mystics, such as St John of the Cross, seem to deny the possibility of
founding any knowledge-claims whatever on mystical experiences.

[9] H. H. Price, 'Faith and Belief', in *Faith and the Philosophers*, ed. J. Hick,
pp.3–25.

Price's variant of this line of thought   Price thinks that there is a very specific acquaintance-experience which we can have in our inner life. Having had it, we cannot doubt that we have a kind of awareness of God.[10] It is impossible to describe this experience adequately,[11] but – and this is the point of Price's essay – we can describe clearly a certain practice which leads to the indescribable experience.[12]

This practice is to adopt a certain role – to act as if there was a loving God, a person whom we can address in prayer and who demands of us a life of love towards our fellow-men. Adopting the role of agapaistic man under the guidance of a personal God, we will all of us discern a cognitive ability of which we were not previously aware. We experience an encounter, after which we know that certain sentences in the religious language have a real anchorage, although the existence of this anchorage cannot be empirically verified.

Criticism   The idea that we can distinguish between real and illusory extraordinary experiences by describing a technique by which the real experience is achieved, but not the illusory one, seems in itself defensible. The same applies to the other central idea in Price's essay: the theory that our cognitive ability is dependent, to a certain extent, on our way of life – the roles and attitudes we adopt, the frames of reference we use, etc.[13] We shall return to this point later on. The important problem in a view like Price's is – as I see it – the following. Do its adherents really rely on the testing procedure they prescribe? What would they say if a man were to follow the practice prescribed but fail to have any 'encounter', or have a strong extraordinary experience of acquaintance with a ghost? There are two possible answers. Either they will allow the different

---

[10] Price expresses himself very carefully and tries to avoid the term 'knowledge'. However, he thinks that faith in God does have some cognitive factor in it (op. cit., p.22).

[11] Price, op. cit., p.14.   [12] Note especially Price, op. cit., p.23.

[13] The theory that the roles we take up determine what we experience of that which is possible to experience is a central idea in the psychological study of Hjalmar Sundén referred to above.

experiences as evidence against their own knowledge-claims, or they will declare the man in question god-blind, not serious, etc. Price seems apt to take the latter path.[14] But then the theory cannot solve our problem. To suggest a testing procedure that must be declared unworkable as soon as it fails to give the expected result is to suggest no testing procedure at all. The first answer to the question makes the theory more interesting. But at the same time, any knowledge-claim based on an extraordinary experience must be extremely uncertain.

3. Faith as Interpretation

Presentation of the argument In discussing indirect statements, we mentioned above a kind of theory relevant to the present problem, namely a theory based on such observations as led us to use the concept of 'ambiguous objects'. According to such theories, religious knowledge is a kind of interpretation of certain ambiguous objects or events, and this interpretation involves the supplementation of empirical factors with an element of an entirely different kind. These theories go on to claim that reasonable arguments may exist for the standpoint that the religious interpretation is the true one, or at least the most adequate. The religious interpretation, according to this view, contains statements relating to something non-empirical. These are statements of the problematic set and the argument – if correct – indicates a method by which we can judge their truth.

There are several versions of the argument. Some of them are linked with the later Wittgenstein and with Wisdom. Let us select and discuss two representative members of this family of arguments.[15]

Faith as experiencing-as according to Hick We will begin with

[14] For example Price, op. cit., p.20.

[15] Interesting commentaries to the theories are to be found in J. Richmond, *Theology and Metaphysics*. By stressing the explanatory character of religious theories Richmond sometimes comes close to the point of view maintained in this chapter.

J. Hick's article 'Religious faith as experiencing-as'.[16] This is not a complete argument, since he does not spell out the reasons for the standpoint that an interpretation which incorporates a non-empirical element may be correct.[17] However, it is interesting as far as it goes. Hick says that all kinds of experience contain an interpretative element. This element seems to be what we have called 'finding a *Gestalt*'. Hick starts his discussion by referring to Wittgenstein's use of the duck-rabbit example in his remarks about seeing-as. He then argues that the kind of interpretation which is apparent when we say that we see a drawing as a rabbit can obviously be found in other kinds of experience than seeing. We can talk about hearing-as, etc. Similarly, we can talk about the total experience of the events of our life or of human history as experience-as. In this case, too, the same interpretative element is present. In our terminology, this means that the events of our life or of human history are ambiguous objects. This, of course, is to expound the notion of seeing-as, but Hick does not stop at this point. He thinks that what he calls experiencing-as involves a kind of interpretation which is always present in all experience, although we are not always conscious of it. Our way of experiencing is not a simple registration which is given once-for-all. 'To recognize or identify is to experience-as in terms of a concept; and our concepts are social products having their life within a particular linguistic environment.'[18]

Having argued that all experience is experiencing-as, he claims that religious experience is a special form of experiencing-as – for example, the experiencing of certain ambiguous events as acts of God. Religious experience thereby emerges as a kind of experience similar in character to all other experiences.

According to Hick the non-empirical element – the acting God – is nothing which is inferred. Speaking about the Old Testament prophets, he says: 'It is, I think, important to realize that this prophetic interpretation of Hebrew history was not in the first place a philosophy of history, a theoretical pattern

16 *Talk of God*, pp.20–35.   17 Hick, op. cit., p.35.
18 Hick, op. cit., p.25. Cf. F. Ferré, *Language, Logic and God*, p.160.

imposed retrospectively upon remembered or recorded events. It was in the first place the way in which the great prophets actually experienced and participated in these events at the time. Hosea did not *infer* Jahweh's mercy; Second Isaiah did not *infer* his universal sovereignty; Jeremiah did not *infer* his holy righteousness – rather they were conscious of the Eternal as acting towards them, and towards their nation, in his mercy, in his holy righteousness, in his absolute sovereignty. They were, in other words, experiencing-as.'[19]

Hick also has an interesting argument which concerns levels of recognition, and different dispositional states connected with different types of interpretation.[20] This is of great importance for the relation between description, ethics, and religion, but it is unfortunately beyond the scope of our present discussion.

At the end of his essay, Hick says that the kind of interpretation that the religious man makes, and which results in statements about God and his acts, may be a veridical interpretation.

F. Ferré's version   The next example of this family of arguments will be taken from the concluding pages of Frederick Ferré's *Language, Logic and God.*

Ferré, like Hick, thinks that there is an interpretative element in all experience. He talks about 'creative powers of intelligence'.[21] He also sees this element as bound up with concept-formation. There is a conceptual scheme in our culture which is well established, and about which we all agree. It is, therefore, possible to speak of ordinary 'facts' and agree about them. However, the creative power of our mind also tries to form a coherent scheme of all the facts, some kind of total view of our situation in the world. This activity, according to Ferré, gives rise to metaphysical systems. Metaphysical knowledge is thus different from non-metaphysical, but – according to both Ferré

---

[19] Hick, op. cit., p.32. Cf. J. Baillie, who writes: 'It is not the result of an inference of any kind, whether explicit or implicit, whether laboriously excogitated or swiftly intuited, that the knowledge of God's reality comes to us' (*Our Knowledge of God*, p.143).

[20] Hick, op. cit., pp. 28ff.   [21] Ferré, op. cit., p.161.

and Hick – there is a continuity; this because the interpretative or creative element, which is striking in the case of metaphysics, is present in all kinds of knowing and experiencing. Ferré now thinks that a metaphysical system often demands the introduction of a new kind of fact, metaphysical facts. He says: 'When we speak of metaphysical "facts", therefore, we need not suppose that these are "given" independent of the creative powers of intelligence. On the contrary, the "facts" of metaphysics are supremely dependent on the conceptual activity of mind. The nature of metaphysics, I suggest, is *conceptual synthesis*. A metaphysical system is a construct of concepts designed to provide coherence for all "the facts" on the basis of a theoretical model drawn from among "the facts". A "metaphysical fact", therefore, is a concept which plays a key role within the system, without which the system would founder.'[22] We have here the introduction of the non-empirical element which is necessary for the formation of the entire scheme. Ferré, unlike Hick, does not stress that the metaphysical facts are immediately experienced. Neither does he explicitly say that the process of constructing a metaphysical system has anything to do with the process we have called finding a certain *Gestalt*; he comes, however, very close to this train of thought.[23]

Ferré discusses briefly the criteria for a correct or adequate metaphysical system. He hints at a testing procedure for such systems. He thinks that metaphysical systems can be found, in differing degree, to 'illuminate' our experience. This he calls the 'applicability to experience'. The correct or perfect metaphysical system is now that which is applicable to all possible experience. Ferré says: 'A conceptual synthesis must not only be applicable to some experience which it interprets; it must (much more demandingly) be adequate to *all* possible experience, if it is to succeed in being of unlimited generality; that is, it must show all experience to be interpreted without oversight, distortion, or "explaining away" on the basis of its key concepts.'[24]

22 Ferré, op. cit., p.161.
23 Cf. Ferré, op. cit., p.157.
24 Ferré, op. cit., p.163.

Comments on the arguments   Let us now interpret and discuss these arguments, using the terminology introduced on p.45. Their common starting-point can be interpreted as the circumstance that important objects of experience are ambiguous objects. This seems to me to be a reasonable view. Examples of such objects are human nature, society, the history of mankind, the empirical universe as a whole. We thus have a kind of disagreement (for example, between behaviourists and existentialists, Marxists and liberals, materialists and dualists) which cannot be solved by an appeal to facts.[25]

For the argument to work we must also assume that these ambiguous objects are objects with an uncertain *Gestalt* and not with a changing *Gestalt*. This important distinction is not generally observed. The argument as it stands, therefore, does not lead to the conclusion that one of the possible interpretations may be the correct one. If the ambiguous objects in question are objects with a changing *Gestalt*, then religious interpretations cannot result in true statements. The truth is simply that the entity can be experienced as a . . ., or as a . . ., or as a . . ., where the religious view has to be inserted as one of the alternatives. However, we could add to the argument the assumption that the objects giving rise to a religious interpretation are objects with an uncertain *Gestalt*. Is this assumption reasonable? It is very difficult to see what reasons can be given for it, and to neglect this point is a serious gap in the argument.[26]

What, then, of the idea that the interpretative element is present in all kinds of experience? This is a very far-reaching idea which can be developed in many directions. We can think of Kant's theory of categories, Marx's theory of base and superstructure, Habermas' sociology of knowledge, to mention only three. It is impossible to adopt a position on all these

[25] Cf. Hick, op. cit., p.26. Cf. also what Wisdom calls 'Connecting Technique' in 'Gods', *Philosophy and Psycho-Analysis*, pp.159ff. See for a commentary J. Richmond, *Theology and Metaphysics*, pp.60ff.

[26] Cf. J. S. K. Ward, 'Existence, Transcendence and God', *Religious Studies* 3, 1968, p.466.

ideas in a few lines. It would be extremely helpful if the theory could be so designed as to eliminate the necessity of adopting a definite position in this general field of epistemology. This, however, seems difficult if the argument is to follow the lines laid down by Hick and Ferré. A risk in their way of connecting religious and scientific experience is that the great difference between these two kinds of experience will disappear, and that they will have difficulty in explaining the widespread unity noticeable in science compared with the striking disunity apparent in religious and metaphysical matters.

The crucial step in the argument is to explain how an interpretation can provide some kind of supplementation of the empirical factors of the situation experienced. This must be something typical of religious interpretations. Hick talks of experiencing certain situations as acts of God. If such an experience leads us to formulate statements of the problematic set, it must involve the introduction of a non-empirical element – namely an acting God. Where does the idea of a God come from? Here the theory that all experience is 'experience-as' is helpful to Hick. If all experience contains an interpretation with the help of concepts, then it must somehow be possible to get an appropriate conceptual apparatus, and to learn to recognize things and events as chairs, war, etc. The manner in which this becomes possible, says Hick, is mysterious. He continues: 'We have learned, starting from scratch, to identify rabbits and forks and innumerable other kinds of things. And so there is thus far in principle no difficulty about the claim that we may learn to use the concept "act of God", as we have learned to use other concepts, and acquire the capacity to recognize exemplifying instances.'[27]

This is not a very good argument. First, it explains our difficulties in recognizing the acts of God by referring to similar difficulties in all experiences. These difficulties may be the result of interpreting all experiences in a way which makes them parallel to religious experiences. It may be possible to meet this first objection. Secondly, however, Hick ignores the difference

[27] Hick, op. cit., p.27.

between seeing something as a rabbit and seeing an event as an act of God; the latter involves the introduction not only of a new concept but of a new entity or ontological category, namely God. If this is not the case, then sentences about God cannot be statements with a localization in the real world. Further, how can we immediately experience something as something else which involves a new existence-claim? Hick seems to me to oscillate between interpretation as a specific organization of the various elements and as the introduction of some new principle. As regards his example of the prophets, we can say that even if a prophet believes himself to experience immediately the acts of God, we cannot exclude the possibility that what he takes to be an immediate experience may be an unconscious inference or explanation, and perhaps a false one.

Ferré speaks explicitly of metaphysical 'facts', but he says very little about how we come to assume these facts. He thinks that they are somehow felt to be necessary for the ordering of our total empirical experience. We can here formulate an idea which may, perhaps, be an interpretation of both Hick and Ferré, as follows. Some of the possible *Gestalts* of an ambiguous object are more than an organization of the empirical elements of which the object consists. The *Gestalt* cannot be experienced without supplying the empirical elements with a factor of an entirely different kind.[28] This kind of *Gestalt* is then found to be the most adequate one by many persons. I am not sure that this is a clear idea which is applicable to religious sentences. It seems difficult to imagine that the introduction of new entities like gods can be seen in analogy with the completion of an incomplete image to make a closed *Gestalt*. The

[28] R. W. Hepburn has clearly criticized some arguments similar to the ones discussed here in his essay 'Poetry and Religious Belief', included in Toulmin, Hepburn, MacIntyre, *Metaphysical Beliefs*. Discussing arguments for a transcendent God Hepburn shows that the completion of vague and ambiguous figures by our imagination or the forming of new patterns cannot be totally substituted for some kind of inference-patterns like the ones belonging to the cosmological or teleological arguments (op. cit., pp.127ff., esp. p.129).

religious completing activity seems to be more like some kind of inference or explanation, as observed by the Thomistic and other classical theories.

The final step in the argument is to argue that there is a testing procedure by which we can establish which of the possible *Gestalts* is the most adequate. This procedure is then one of the M:s in premise (ii) of the argument on p.32. If it shows that a religious interpretation is correct, we can make statements of the problematic kind withoug falling foul of the general argument against such statements. Following Ferré, we can formulate the method in our terminology as follows: if the object of study is an ambiguous entity with an uncertain *Gestalt*, try to find as many alternative *Gestalts* as possible, including those which involve a supplementation of the situation with a new kind of element. Choose as the correct *Gestalt* that which is experienced as most adequate. But if we add to the principles of choice between different possible interpretations the principle of economy – Occam's razor[29] – then we can easily see that the situation of religious statements is not very promising. Is Occam's razor a reasonable principle to use here? We shall return to this question below.

We have seen that there are interesting tendencies in this line of argument. However, it has many weak points. It does not observe the distinction between an object with a changing *Gestalt* and one with an uncertain *Gestalt*; consequently, it ignores the difficulty of discriminating between them.[30] Even after our attempts to make these suggestions more precise,

[29] The principle is traditionally formulated: *entia praeter necessitatem non esse multiplicanda.*

[30] Some philosophers who have criticized similar arguments seem to have noticed the difficulties which we have tried to make explicit here. See John Macquarrie, *Twentieth-Century Religious Thought*, SCM Press, London 1963, p.316. James Richmond, who comments on Macquarrie's argument and a similar one from H. D. Lewis in his *Theology and Metaphysics*, pp.87ff., is also aware of the problem. However, he points out that Lewis' and Macquarrie's argument does not exactly touch Hick's theory. If Lewis and Macquarrie are interpreted as having seen the difficulty explained in our text, the most important point in their criticism is not refuted by Richmond's argument on p.88.

there remains some lack of clarity concerning the supplementation of empirical facts with non-empirical factors.
Finally, the principles for the choice between different metaphysical or religious interpretations involve many problems
which have been insufficiently observed.

4. *A theory illustrating the ultimate choices in judging religious language*

We now come to the last part of this book. We shall here endeavour to show what choices, and what kinds of choice, we
have to make if we want to adopt the position that some religious
sentences of the problematic set are statements with a localization in the real world. We shall here utilize some ideas from
the preceding arguments which we have found to be sound.

Ambiguous objects   As a starting-point, we will take the notion
of ambiguous objects. We said above that it seems reasonable
to claim that certain important objects of our inquiry may be
ambiguous objects. We gave some examples, and mentioned
that the idea of ambiguous objects has an explanatory force.
It can explain a kind of disagreement which seems to be
unavoidable even among scientifically educated men.[31]

However, to say that human history, for instance, is an

---

[31] If we take up the view that the empirical universe as a whole emerges
as having a changing *Gestalt* when we try to think about it, then it is no
great step to think that different metaphysical systems consist of different
sets of ideas or concepts with which we think about the world as a whole.
This is a theory about metaphysics similar to the theories suggested by G. J.
Warnock (in his contribution to *The Revolution in Philosophy*, Macmillan,
London 1956, pp.120ff.) and P. F. Strawson (*Individuals*, Methuen, London
1959). M. Charlesworth has called it the 'alternative-language view'
('Metaphysics as Conceptual Revision', *The Philosophical Quarterly* XVI,
1966, pp.308–18; cf. Ferré's 'conceptual synthesis', op. cit., p.161). Charlesworth formulates a strong argument against some forms of this view of
metaphysics. His argument, however, does not touch the view of religious
statements outlined in our text. Cf. David Pole, who says: 'A new way of
thinking or speaking corresponds, on the ontological side, to the emergence
of a new aspect' (' "Languages" and Aspects of Things', *The Philosophical
Quarterly* XII, 1962, p.314). An illustration of the attempt of religious men
to find in certain moments a *Gestalt* in the surrounding world is given by
Ninian Smart, *Reasons and Faiths*, p.40.

ambiguous object is a loose way of speaking. There is naturally much to be said about history which is the result of ordinary research. The same, of course, is true of human nature or the universe. The point is that certain properties of these objects are dependent on one of many possible organizations of the data given by scholarly work, and it cannot be decided by further research which organization is the most adequate. Some of these organizations can easily assimilate new data, and there seem to be contradictory interpretations which can never be resolved by empirical research. The different *Gestalts* can, however, influence science, in that they may guide the interest of the scientist in different directions. Non-scientific views of the world, such as dialectical or historical materialism, have influenced social scientists in a direction which has given new scientific results.

There is also another connection between science and what, at any given time, seems to be one of the possible ways of experiencing an ambiguous object. It can be the case that new facts render one organization impossible. The border-line between interpretations of ambiguous objects and ordinary scientific experience is therefore not sharp. This can be studied in the development of world-views and cosmological theories.[32]

Two kinds of explanatory hypothesis   Our next step is to distinguish between two different kinds of explanatory hypothesis or theory. The first kind is the scientific explanatory hypothesis. Such a hypothesis or theory can loosely be said to point out the antecedents of the objects to be explained, and to identify the principles which connect the antecedent with the *explanandum*. This principle is often expressed in a law or law-like sentence. The objects which form the basis of the theory or hypothesis will in a certain sense be public, i.e. everyone will be able to perceive them in the appropriate circumstances. We can qualify what has just been said in a number of ways.[33] This is a question

[32] See, for instance, Stephen Toulmin, *Foresight and Understanding*, Hutchinson, London 1961.

[33] A qualification of the concept of fact is made by J. Wisdom and his followers. See R. Bambrough, *Reason, Truth and God*, Chapter 4. It is such

for the philosophy of science. What we have said is at a common-sense level, and we need not go into it any further for our present purpose. As a result of applying a correct scientific explanatory hypothesis, we experience order and connection between separate objects; and sometimes the hypothesis will make it possible to forecast new developments in the objects in question.

We shall distinguish from the scientific explanatory hypothesis what we may term 'non-scientific' hypotheses. The difference does not lie in the kind of explanation which the hypotheses provide, but in the objects they explain. In this case they are ambiguous objects. Different people having an exhaustive knowledge of the same observational situation can disagree as to the correct description of these objects. If, now, important objects of knowledge really are ambiguous objects of this kind, then it is quite natural that we should seek explanations also in this field. We try to find a theory that will provide an order among the ambiguous objects, and which may give us an opportunity to make predictions. However, the theory or hypothesis in question cannot be a scientific one, since the data on which it is based are impossible in principle to describe in a manner upon which all men can agree.

Thesis   We can now return to the religious sentences of the problematic set. It seems possible that many of these sentences express non-scientific explanatory hypotheses. For example: 'God created the world.' 'Yahweh is the Lord of history.' 'The principle of reincarnation determines the course of the world.' 'God takes care of every human individual.' 'Muhammed was the apostle of God.'[34]

---

that it makes the border-line less sharp between ambiguous and non-ambiguous objects. It is, however, a great exaggeration to say that the distinction has been shown to be irrelevant.

[34] Cf. on this and what is said below about the place of analogies and metaphors, Alston, 'The Elucidation of Religious Statements', *Process and Divinity*, esp. p.442. The explanatory character of Christian doctrine is stressed by G. F. Woods in his book *Theological Explanation*, James Nisbet and Co., Welwyn 1958, for example on p.155. However, the main argument of that book differs from ours. Bochenski, who also underlines the

Faith, according to Hick, is the interpretation of ambiguous objects. According our present theory, it is both interpretation and explanation. The supposition that some important religious sentences of the problematic set are non-scientific hypotheses is itself a hypothesis of the scientific kind and, if a good one, will at least connect up the various observations we have made

---

importance of explanatory hypotheses among basic religious sentences, comes closer to our point. See his *The Logic of Religion*, pp.148ff. A. MacIntyre has argued that the provisional and tentative adherence which is typical of adherence to a hypothesis is completely uncharacteristic of religious belief. He writes: 'To hold Christian belief as a hypothesis would be to render it no longer Christian belief' ('The Logical Status of Religious Belief' in Toulmin, Hepburn, MacIntyre, *Metaphysical Beliefs*, p.181). MacIntyre's argument is taken up by Kai Nielsen, 'Christian Positivism and the Appeal to Religious Experience', *Journal of Religion* XLII, 1962, pp.26of. Cf. also J. Kellenberger, 'The Falsification Challenge', *Religious Studies* 5, 1969, pp.75f. This argument is, according to my view, correctly refuted by Basil Mitchell referring to Bishop Butler (Basil Mitchell, 'The Justification of Religious Belief', *The Philosophical Quarterly* XI, 1961, pp.217f.). Cf. also Bochenski, loc. cit. and Thomas McPherson, 'The Falsification Challenge: A Comment', *Religious Studies* 5, 1969, p.82. Our conclusion in this chapter, however, has a likeness to MacIntyre's view in so far as it stresses the importance of decisions beyond rational argumentation for a person who wishes to embrace a religious faith. But the ultimate decisions lie on a different level according to our theory, and we can therefore give more room for arguments in questions of religious truth. In accordance with Mitchell we can say that there can be rational choices between world views (Mitchell, op. cit., p.226). See below and cf. the debate about 'Wittgensteinian fideism' between Kai Nielsen and W. D. Hudson in *Philosophy* XLII, 1967, pp.191–209; XLIII, 1968, pp.269–73; XLIV, 1969, pp. 63–6.

The thesis in Chapter V runs contrary to a main line in Wittgenstein's later philosophy, in spite of its connection to Wittgensteinian thought, but I cannot find that the few arguments from Wittgenstein himself or the more elaborate arguments of such philosophers as D. Z. Philips are conclusive against my view. The supposition that statements of the kind exemplified are non-scientific explanatory hypotheses does not say how religious men have come to know them. The thesis does not exclude that religious people have come to know some of them through a revelation. It is also logically possible to combine our theory with the theological idea that the full Christian faith is a gift from God.

Not all non-scientific religious hypotheses are religious, of course. See the comparison between religious theories and the theories of the early Greek philosophers provided by Ben Kimpel in his *The Symbols of Religious Faith*, Philosophical Library, New York 1954, pp.105ff.

concerning the problematic set of sentences. Let us now discuss briefly how far this is the case.

The relation between the thesis and the preceding observations of religious statements   A defining characteristic of a sentence of the problematic set is that it cannot be falsified by science. This can be true of a non-scientific explanatory hypothesis because some of the ambiguous objects which it explains seem to be such that the experience of them is not influenced by new facts. The similarity, noted by Flew, Heimbeck and others, between the sentences in question and scientific hypotheses becomes clear in our interpretation, and we can also explain the fact that the border-line between scientific hypotheses and sentences of the problematic set is unclear to persons lacking a scientific edcuation.[35]

We have noted that it can sometimes, when new scientific discoveries are made, become difficult for religious people to go on believing in a sentence which seems to belong to the problematic set, and that some philosophers therefore deny that religious sentences like those on p.122 above belong to the problematic set. This situation is one that could be expected if these sentences were non-scientific explanatory hypotheses. The experience of the ambiguous objects which they explain is, as noted above, not always entirely resistant to new facts. It may become impossible to uphold one of the conceivable *Gestalts*

[35] In his *Reason, Truth and God*, R. Bambrough has taken up the point of view that – however great the differences are – there is still a family resemblance between the use of religious sentences by Homer, for instance, and among Christian believers today. He therefore thinks – rightly, according to my view – that we can learn much about present-day religious language by studying the similarities and differences between our modern language and the language of Homer. In discussing the sentence 'Poseidon is angry' (p.30), Bambrough says that it probably could have been used as an explanation of a meteorological fact. As such it does not belong to the problematic set as falsified. When we classify some important religious sentences as non-scientific explanatory hypotheses we easily see their likeness to religious sentences important to Homer: their explanatory character. And at the same time the fundamental difference emerges: the corresponding present-day sentences belong to the problematic set and are scientifically unfalsifiable.

when further scientific knowledge of the object appears. This, however, does not exclude the possibility that some experiences of some events of the kind exemplified may be resistant, as far as we know, to further scientific knowledge, and that sentences used in the explanation of such events really can belong to the problematic set. Metaphysical materialism, as well as the belief in a Creator, seems to be of this kind.

As we found in Chapter II, untranslatable metaphors and indirect sentences are of great importance in religious language, and we have shown a possible way in which they may work. One main function was to evoke and express one of the possible experiences of ambiguous objects. This observation is in accordance with the theory that some religious sentences of the problematic set are non-scientific explanatory hypotheses. Descriptions of ambiguous entities are then of decisive importance in religion.

If the non-scientific hypothesis is the supposition of a transcendent reality, it is easy to understand the important place in religious philosophy which must be ascribed to such constructions as Bultmann's and Tillich's, or to the theory of analogy.

According to the view we exemplified from H. H. Price, there is a certain way of living which we can point to and which leads to certain indescribable experiences. Thus far, Price's observation seems to be empirically true. We can connect it with the present line of thought in two ways. First, a certain way of living – the adoption of certain roles – can determine our experiences of ambiguous objects and thereby affect our non-scientific explanatory hypotheses. Secondly, the overwhelming experiences of a totally different reality which some religious men report, when they live according to certain rules, are themselves data which we must take into account when trying to find a *Gestalt* in the ambiguous universe in which we live. They may fit into a picture of the universe which confirms the non-scientific explanatory hypotheses of a materialist metaphysics, but we must then deny that they are experiences of something real – in spite of the overwhelming reality-experience with which they often are connected. The theistic hypothesis explains the occurrence of such experiences and makes it possible to say that they are experiences of something real. This is a circumstance which may sustain the theistic hypothesis.[36] We noted certain general difficulties confronting those who claim, on the basis of religious experiences, that sentences of the problematic set are true statements. These difficulties do not confront to the same degree those who introduce religious experiences as one among many circumstances which confirm a theistic non-scientific explanatory hypothesis.

Having seen that the observations of Price are consistent with the theory of non-scientific explanatory hypotheses, we can also, on the basis of this theory, recognize the importance of circumstantial metaphors in religion. If there is an indescribable experience, and a certain way of living leads to that experience, then it seems reasonable to try to talk about such an experience metaphorically by talking about the situation in which it occurs, i.e. by circumstantial metaphors.

If we interpret a religious sentence of the problematic set as a non-scientific explanatory hypothesis, it becomes possible to explain the process of introducing a new kind of entity. We can here rightly use the often misused parallel between the supposition of non-observable particles in physics and the supposition of an indescribable God.[37] Both have an explanatory force, but in different fields.

[36] A similar point is made in my *Filosofisk Religionsdebatt* (Philosophical Debate on Religion), Verbum, Stockholm 1967, p.77 and in Richmond, op. cit., pp.96f.

[37] For a critique of the parallel see A. MacIntyre, 'The Logical Status of Religious Belief', Toulmin, Hepburn, MacIntyre, *Metaphysical Beliefs*, p.196. It is possible to accept MacIntyre's critical remarks and at the same time adhere to our line of thought here. In arguing against the reasonableness of supposing a transcendent reality in theology R. Bambrough says: 'The transcendentalist theologian is tempted to buy his immunity from refutation at the exorbitant price of a total failure to say anything about the world we know. It seems to make no difference to anything in our world whether God exists or not' (*Reason, Truth and God*, p.52). This, however, does not refute a person who supposes some transcendent reality as a non-scientific explanatory hypothesis. (Our book contains only the beginning of a discussion of the problems of transcendence. For a fuller treatment one can find interesting viewpoints in Bambrough, op. cit., Chapter 6.)

Having accepted a certain non-scientific hypothesis – for example the existence of a Creator – we can experience immediately the world as a creation, as described by Hick. Perhaps we can also find parallels to this circumstance in the scientific field.

Testing a non-scientific hypothesis: an example It may be necessary at this point to spell out how a testing procedure for a non-scientific explanatory hypothesis can be performed (the M in premise (ii) of the argument on p.32). Let us imagine that I reflect upon human life, upon everything I have felt and learnt about it. I find that I can see it in different ways. The facts of life can fall into different patterns. I thus confront different hypotheses which aim to explain this complex whole.[38] One says that human life is a result of the dialectical movement of matter. Another says that there is a loving God who created every man and who wants to lead him to eternal happiness. I find that there are possible *Gestalts* of human life which can confirm both these hypotheses, but I can feel one pattern to be more adequate than the other.[39] One of the hypotheses, therefore, seems the more probable. For further testing, I work out the pattern which the future of human life can be expected to assume according to the different hypotheses, and in the course of time I try to establish which fits my experience the more adequately. The predictions involved, however, cannot relate to scientifically determinable events. In such a case the hypothesis would change its character and become scientific or quasi-scientific. After a time I might perhaps find that one of the hypotheses explains human life. It gives to the stream of events a pattern which I feel to be adequate. The new facts fall into this pattern in a way which I can expect. When I

[38] Cf. the following quotation from David Pole: 'The history of metaphysics might be thought of as a series of experiments in ways of seeing the world – as an endless flux, a single coherent and intelligible unity or a vast concourse of atoms in motion' (' "Languages" and Aspects of Things', *The Philosophical Quarterly* XII, 1962, p.313).

[39] Cf. the observations of H. H. Price concerning the use of 'adequate' in judging about 'world-outlooks' in his article 'Belief "in" and Belief "that" ', *Religious Studies* 1, 1965, p.9.

express the experiences of life against which I test the hypotheses, and when I work out the hypotheses, I use language
metaphorically or indirectly in a way which can be explained
by the theories we have discussed.

A characteristic trait of the religious explanatory hypothesis
is that it aims to explain the empirical universe as a whole,
including scientific activity.[40] Such hypotheses thus acquire a
kind of ultimate character, and, if they contain an existence-
claim, it is easy to understand that the kind of reality which is
supposed is often claimed to be of a different kind from anything else in the universe, i.e. it is something transcendent.
When a non-scientific hypothesis is directed towards the universe as a whole, Ferré's observations become relevant for the
testing of it: 'It must show all experience to be interpreted
without oversight, distortion, or "explaining away" on the
basis of its key concepts.'[41]

*Ultimate decisions necessary to determine the status of religious non-
scientific hypotheses*   If, now, it is correct that some important
religious sentences of the problematic set are non-scientific
explanatory hypotheses, is our main question answered? If we
have succeeded in proving these sentences to be non-scientific
explanatory hypotheses, have we then shown them to be true or
false statements with a localization in the real world? The
answer unfortunately is: not at all. There are two crossroads at
which we have to choose one of the possible alternatives, before
we can arrive at such a standpoint.

The first choice is one which was relevant also to the line
of thought we examplified from Hick and Ferré. It concerns
the *Gestalt* of the ambiguous objects. If the *Gestalt* is a changing
one, a hypothesis which explains the event experienced in one
of many equally adequate but quite different ways cannot be
true. Are, then, the events which are explained by the non-
scientific hypothesis events with a changing *Gestalt* or with an

[40] See further Anders Jeffner, *Butler and Hume on Religion*, pp.164ff, 239ff.
and Ninian Smart, *Reasons and Faiths*, pp.36–8.
[41] Ferré, op. cit., p.163.

uncertain *Gestalt*? In other words, is there a way of experiencing our situation as men in the world which is true? Here I think we meet the first crossroad, at which reasons in the ordinary sense of the word cannot help us in our choice. There is no kind of investigation which can show us if our way of organizing the elements in our situation is one among several equally true organizations of the available data, or if one of the possible *Gestalts* is more adequate than the others.

To choose the first alternative is the move of the metaphysical pessimist. The metaphysical pessimist can rely on the results of psychology, historical research and natural science, and he can find religious and metaphysical systems interesting and beautiful, but he denies that any one of them can be true. They resemble only different interpretations of a Rorschach blot. The world can only be understood to a certain limited extent, and the limits are the limits of science. According to the second alternative, there is a truth about man and the world which goes far beyond the limits of science. Whether or not we have it or can now reach it, there is one view of my own life, of the life of mankind, or of the universe, which is correct. Therefore we can also hope to find certain hypotheses which will make it possible to understand and explain our total situation. To take this side is the move of the metaphysical optimist.

The choice between metaphysical pessimism and optimism cannot be theoretically justified, but we have to choose. This seems to be one of the genuine free choices spoken of by the existentialists.

The second decisive question is as follows: is it a reasonable task to seek non-scientific explanations? In other words: is it or is it not a praiseworthy attitude to be content with science and common sense, and to suspend our judgment in the field to which the non-scientific explanations belong? It is logically possible to be a metaphysical optimist, but to answer this question in the negative. Even in this case, it is difficult (or rather impossible) to give any reasons for choosing a particular side. We have to choose one, and I cannot see that the one is more rational than the other.

There is a third question of the same type that must be asked by everyone who thinks of accepting a religious non-scientific hypothesis which involves a new existence-claim, for example the existence of a God. If it is possible – which it often may be – to find another hypothesis by which we can explain the world without introducing a new ontological category, ought we not, on the principle of economy, to prefer this hypothesis? Is it possible to apply Occam's Razor in the field of non-scientific explanations, in the same manner as in science? In science we can give certain reasons for it. It has proved fruitful. However, the same cannot be claimed in the case of non-scientific explanations. Further, it is not at all clear that this principle means here. What, for example, is 'necessary'? There may be situations in which a metaphysical optimist accepting non-scientific explanations will find a theistic hypothesis justified even if he subscribes to the principle of economy. But if the choice between two hypotheses depends only on the acceptance or rejection of Occam's Razor, there seems to be a choice of the same ultimate character as the two preceding.

We can imagine a person who makes such choices in these matters that he is a metaphysical optimist finding the belief in a life after death to be part of a reasonable non-scientific explanatory hypothesis. This person can hope to come to know that he was right in his ultimate decisions. The theory of eschatological verification, therefore, can be of importance in adopting a position towards the problematic set of sentences, although its adherents generally expect too much of it.

The character of these decisions   In these three last questions, we seem to be in a normative meta-theoretical field. We have to make a decision in regard to three ultimate norms. The first says that we ought to see the world as ultimately understandable; the second that we ought to accept certain non-scientific explanations; the third prescribes how we ought to choose between explanations. In ethics, I think, we encounter certain basic norms, which we simply have to accept or reject and which we cannot give any further reasons for or against. If we are right here, an analogous situation exists in the theoretical field. We can regret this situation, but we cannot alter it.

Sentences of the problematic set   If we adopt the optimist's move and also try to find a non-scientific explanation – something which most people seem to do, consciously or unconsciously – we have opened the door for a legitimate use of religious language which is in accordance with its factual use among religious men. We can make truth-claims for problematic sentences and see them as statements, with a localization in the real world.

If we take the other roads, this is impossible.

INDEX OF NAMES

Albrecht, R., 58
Aldrich, V. C., 110
Aldwinckle, R. F., 49
Alston, W. P., 11, 16, 56, 122
Aquinas, 53, 55, 77, 78
Aristotle, 83
Austin, J. L., 99

Baillie, J., 108, 114
Bambrough, R., 20, 121, 124, 126
Bartsch, H. W., 61
Beardsley, M. C., 44
Bejerholm, L., 88, 89, 93, 100, 101, 102, 103
Bell, R. H., 8
Black, M., 44, 45, 46, 48, 53, 61
Blackstone, W. T., 4, 7, 13, 33, 34, 107
Bochenski, J. M., 7, 20, 30, 31, 105, 122, 123
Bock, I., 64
Braithwaite, R. B., 5, 7, 22, 33, 35, 38, 39, 42, 43, 75
Brandt, R. B., 76
Brown, S. C., 63
Buber, M., 108, 110
Bultmann, R., 27, 28, 29, 39, 60, 61, 62, 63, 64, 106, 125
van Buren, P., 75, 78, 79, 80, 102
Butler, J., 123

Charlesworth, M., 120
Chisholm, R. M., 12, 99, 100
Christian, W. A., 9, 29, 88

Coburn, R. C., 48
Copleston, F., 78
Cox, D., 33
Crombie, I. M., 35, 43, 107

Donaldson, D. M., 83

Ewing, A. C., 75, 108

al-Fárábí, 83
Farmer, H. H., 108
Ferré, F., 13, 47, 113, 114, 115, 117, 118, 119, 120, 128
Flew, A., 3, 6, 20, 22, 23, 27, 30, 32, 33, 34, 108, 124
Frank, E., 64
Freud, S., 69, 82

Gerhardsson, B., 37
Gibb, H. A. R., 36, 42
Goodman, N., 6
Grass, H., 7, 8
Gyllenkrok, A., 76

Habermas, J., 116
Hedenius, I., 91, 92
Heidegger, M., 63, 85
Heimbeck, R. S., 20, 22, 23, 24, 25, 26, 124
Hepburn, R. W., 32, 33, 34, 48, 108, 118, 123, 126
Hick, J., 49, 88, 107, 110, 112, 113, 114, 115, 116, 117, 118, 119, 123, 127, 128
High, D. M., 47

Homer, 124

Hook, S., 58

Hornig, G., 88, 89, 93, 100, 101, 102, 103

Hosea, 114

Hospers, J., 15

Hudson, W. D., 123

Hutchinson, J. A., 34

Iqbāl, M., 42

Isaiah, 77, 114

James, W., 9

Jeffner, A., 56, 126, 128

Jephthah, 90, 92, 94

Jeremiah, 114

Jesus Christ, 6, 21, 23, 24, 30, 36, 37, 48, 50, 53, 78, 84, 86, 93, 101

St John of the Cross, 110

Joseph, 24

Kant, I., 116

Kellenberger, J., 123

Kimpel, B., 123

Lewis, H. D., 119

Luther, M., 61

Lyas, C., 11, 18

MacIntyre, A., 6, 48, 108, 118, 123, 126

MacKinnon, A., 34

McPherson, T., 23, 123

Macquarrie, J., 50, 61, 119

Martin, C. B., 108

Marx, K., 116

Mary, 21

Miles, T. R., 27, 33, 88

Mitchell, B., 1, 24, 35, 43, 107, 123

Mohammed, 3, 6, 21, 86, 122

Morris, C. W., 14

Moses, 21

Möller, J. G., 62

Nielsen, K., 30, 33, 36, 108, 123

Nisbet, J., 122

Occam, W., 119, 130

Osgood, C., 71

Paul, 37, 38

Pedersen, J., 36

Philips, D. Z., 123

Pole, D., 120, 127

Price, H. H., 110, 111, 112, 125, 126, 127

Pufendorf, S., 14

Ramsey, I. T., 8, 48, 49, 53, 61

Reese, W. L., 56

Richards, I. A., 44, 46

Richmond, J., 20, 34, 112, 116, 119, 126

Robinson, N. H. G., 40, 98, 99

Rowe, W. L., 31

Ryle, G., 11, 18

Sartre, J. P., 15

Scott, J. B., 14

Simonsson, T., 5

Smalley, B., 53

Smart, N., 3, 21, 42, 55, 75, 109, 120, 128

Stace, W. T., 42, 56, 110

Stevenson, C. L., 75, 76

Strawson, P. F., 120

Streng, F. J., 42, 85

Suci, G. J., 71

Sundén, H., 69, 111

Tannenbaum, P. H., 71

Tillich, P., 29, 56, 57, 58, 59, 60, 62, 65, 106, 125

Toulmin, S. E., 48, 118, 121, 123, 126

Urban, W. M., 49

Waismann, F., 56
Ward, J. S. K., 116
Warnock, G. J., 120
Wedberg, A., 66
Wennerberg, H., 9
Williams, B., 6, 7, 8
Wilson, J., 108
Wisdom, J., 20, 112, 116, 121

Wittgenstein, L., 8, 9, 34, 43, 62, 66,
  112, 113, 123
Woods, G. F., 122

Zaehner, R. C., 109
Zola, E., 50
Zurdeeg, W. F., 64, 65, 66